BOAT
FISH
LIVE

#1 RATED BOATING AND FISHING LESSONS
100% HANDS-ON LEARNING EXPERIENCE

BY CAPTAIN BRIAN BRANIGAN

Copyright © 2020-2024 by Brian Branigan

ISBN: 978-0-9892840-2-8

All Rights Reserved. No part of this book may be reproduced in any manner without the express written consent of the author.

Printed in the United States of America

Written by Brian Branigan
Photography by Brian Branigan
Design by Allison Branigan / islanddesign.us

Contact info:
info@keysboattours.com

Websites:
www.boatfishlive.net
www.keysboattours.com

This book proudly abides by the framework of the **Blue Star** program; a Florida Keys National Marine Sanctuary effort recognizing tour operators who are committed to promoting responsible and sustainable diving, snorkeling, and fishing practices to reduce the impact of these activities on ecosystems in the Florida Keys.

www.sanctuarybluestar.org

Dedicated to mentors worldwide, including YouTube mentors without whom I personally would not know how to maintain a motor, much less tie a knot.

———————————

I urge you, the reader, to make use of the educational and constructive contributions of YouTube videos with regards to this book.

PREFACE

Some people come into boating and fishing early in life. Others, not until their mid twenties, or much later. I ran into a childhood friend of mine who had heard about my book, and said, *"I don't remember you as being that into boating when you were young."* I responded, *"That's very observant of you, because I wasn't."*

Many boating and fishing enthusiasts are lucky to be raised and trained in such an environment. Then, there are those who happen upon it later on in life – some not until retirement. I grew up in a boating community of sorts, but even still, boating was foreign to me, or not in my comfort zone. I guess I was intimidated by it at the time.

But, here I am decades later: a USCG certified captain, 50 ton master, owner of a tour boat business, guide, instructor, and author. It demonstrates the surprises that life can throw at you. And, it just goes to prove, that you never stop learning, or evolving, and you just never know where you will end up – or start anew.

I am proud of this book. I hope and believe that it will help many people discover boating and fishing in a way that is otherwise not available to them. It is difficult to come into something late in life. Or, even early in life, especially something like boating and fishing, where there is a sizable investment and a steep learning curve – that period of time where one beats oneself over the head, screaming at your konked out motor, snagged line, and lost leader while you decide whether – or not, you truly enjoy it.

Boating and fishing are two separate activities. Perhaps you enjoy boating and not fishing, or vice versa. Maybe you prefer something altogether different – like art. The point is: I got into something totally unexpected. I reinvented myself, not as a plan, but something perhaps better described as – that crossroad where necessity and opportunity meet. I then archived said experience into a book, this book, **Boat Fish Live**.

My business, Keys Boat Tours, is now the #1 rated recreational tour boat business in the area on TripAdvisor. I am by no means the best guide in the Lower Keys, and I am certainly not among the top fishing guides. I simply take it one tour at a time, as if each tour were my last, and I do my best to make it a memorable experience for the client or passenger(s), not as the highlight of their Keys visit, but hopefully one of many highlights. I then repeat the process for the next tour, lesson, or ride – and keep learning.

The journey to get to where I am today was challenging, for sure. It is still challenging – with each and every outing, some days more challenging than others. But, it is fun too. I first began my tour boat business with a small flats boat, then a medium sized bay boat, then a slightly larger center console boat, and built my way up. Where I lack in one area, I find strength in another. I relate to people who are new to boating and fishing, or just getting into saltwater boating and fishing. I understand what they need to know to get started. *After all, I was once you.* That, in a nutshell, is this book.

No matter where your starting point is in life, one can always redirect oneself and realize another path. That is the "live" in **Boat Fish Live** (rhymes with give). Were you to ask me ten years ago if I ever thought that I'd be a captain, tour guide, fisherman, instructor, and an author on the subject, my definitive answer would be – absolutely not! Yet, here I am. And, here you are. So, never say never. Just say, you never know. Ah, life lessons!

It is my hope that you get a lot out of this book, including learning a life lesson or two along the way. We never know what's on the other end of the hook or beyond the horizon until we cast a line and see for ourselves. Just remember: enjoy the ride, hold on tight, and appreciate the experience. Afterward, perhaps you will share some too – yes, definitely do. Take the time to share your knowledge with others. Of course, if mentoring is not one of your strengths, you can always gift this book and sign it as I would, ... *"Life is a lesson"*

– Captain Brian

ANCHORS AWEIGH

When in the Florida Keys, boat. But, when boating, know. It is the same where you boat – know don't guess. **Boat Fish Live** includes three chapters; **You: Steer It, Anchor It & Dock It**, **You: Trim It, Tack It & Sail It,** and **You: Rig It, Bait It & Catch It.** In the first chapter, beyond the lesson, we introduce you to a couple of crown jewel Lower Keys destinations – and navigate the way too. This is a much needed hands-on lesson for motor boating, sailing, and fishing. We throw several buckets of good information at you, some of which are certain to drip off, so we include a thorough **Q&A** at the end of each chapter. It is not a quiz, but rather a very handy review.

Boat Fish Live is an easy-to-grasp and easy-to-read hands-on boating lesson. The book intentionally side steps technical details of a boating book such as, **Boating Skills and Seamanship** by the United States Coast Guard Auxiliary, a book we highly recommend. Instead, it focuses on real world everyday boating, what you need to know to enjoy a safe day on the water. That said, this hands-on lesson seamlessly dovetails with the USCG Aux book and lesson, so pairing them makes perfect sense. Our approach is one of mentorship; we share with you all that we have learned over the years, and save you time. Whatever your age, 12 or 82+, you will learn to boat with confidence, and experience a positive and lasting memory. The important part is to learn by doing, hands-on. Our approach is one of ethical boating, and habitat conservation practices.

You might be interested in our instructor trainer course. Those who are, have the option to stay. We are located inside Big Pine Key RV, which has very comfortable rental units. Afterward, bring what you've learned back home, and customize the lesson to your area. We have a student lesson for individuals and couples too, with the option of an overnight stay at the resort; one or two days on the water, and one or several nights stay. Each lesson is a half day. What better way to visit the Lower Keys? This hands-on lesson is recommended for one and two students at a time. Kids can join.

You might select just one lesson, or take advantage of all three. There are bits of wisdom to gain from each. Whatever lesson you decide, a minimum 3½ hours of the 4+ hour lesson is 100% hands-on. You are free to add extra time if you choose. At a minimum, the lesson(s) promises to be time well spent, while for others it is perhaps a dream vacation. That is our goal. That, and the 5-star review – that we work hard to earn.

OUR BOAT

The motor boat and fishing lessons are given aboard a 23' center console. It is a Bulls Bay offshore 2300 CC series boat with a four stroke Yamaha 300 hp. Or, it could be your boat. Many students prefer to learn on their own boat – to get more comfortable. And, to put navigation tracks and waypoint marks on their GPS. Whatever your boat of choice, we practice multiple real world situations: rules of the road, anchoring, docking, man overboard, and improvisational readiness. We discuss basic navigation, chart reading, day markers, and introduction to GPS. We also review what equipment you should have on your boat, both required and suggested.

CLASSROOM AND ONLINE LESSONS

The USCG Aux classroom lesson is very useful. We highly recommend it. You might wish to take the classroom lesson or an online class prior to this hands-on lesson, but it is not required for our lesson. It is required that all motorized boat operators born on or after January 1, 1988 must complete an approved boater education course, or pass an approved equivalency exam. This hands-on lesson is not that. But, there is no replacement to learn boating safety, boat operation, local navigation, and the basics of operating, anchoring, and docking a boat hands-on. If you can couple that with an online class, vacation, life goal, or as a gift – perfect! This is your opportunity to boat, navigate, fish, explore, and more.

The most important take-away from the USCG AUX classroom lesson is a philosophy called, the **4-C's**: caution, common sense, consideration of others, and communication. If you follow these basic principles, you are way ahead of the game, in boating – and in life. We put great emphasis on this 4-C concept in our hands-on lesson too. Beyond that, it is awareness of your surroundings and practice that will make the difference. That, and an appreciation for mother nature. Then, comes confidence – but not so much that you defy weather forecasts or take unnecessary risks. Follow up lessons can include additional navigation skills, GPS waypoints and routes, turning in tight spaces, operating twin outboards, motor maintenance, docking practice, trailering technique, or by your request.

YOUR INSTRUCTOR

Captain Brian volunteers as captain at Keys Boat Tours, *keysboattours.com*. He loves meeting new people from different walks of life, and to see them flourish. His wife, Captain Allison, has taken over ownership of the business. Keys Boat Tours is a #1 rated recreational charter boat business on TripAdvisor, and the #1 rated hands-on boat lesson in the Lower Keys. One could say, they even wrote the book on it! Captain Brian has 35+ years experience on the water, with Certificate of Excellence and Travelers' Choice Awards from TripAdvisor. Their hands-on boating and navigation lessons continue to receive rave reviews. Captain Brian has a 50 ton USCG master license with sail and tow endorsements. He is a former Outward Bound instructor, and former captain at Seacamp. Brian is the author of three previous books, **Food Truck 411, The Road To Key West – Marathon To Key West,** and **Once Upon A Timebomb,** a coffee table book on global warming. His next book is based on a 5-day sailing expedition that sets off from Bahia Honda Key to Key West, titled, **Navigating the FL Keys and Finding Yourself**. It is a perspective check journey with an appreciation for adventure. The reader is his boating companion. Brian personally oversees all hands-on lessons at Keys Boat Tours. That is to say, Captain Brian will be your boating mentor (in person) too, unless you prefer Captain Allison aboard her 22' bay boat.

YOU

Our lesson is not so different from any other life goal. You want to push yourself, learn, and fulfill a dream. Whether you are a complete novice, or semi experienced but rusty, you are ready to take the helm, albeit with some supervision. In some cases, if need be, we can come to you – to teach you in your boating playground.

FL 6414 RB

Fixed Bridges
Hor Cl 90ft
Vert Cl 20ft
31
BAHIA HONDA STATE PARK
Ramp
MM 37
Bahia Honda Key

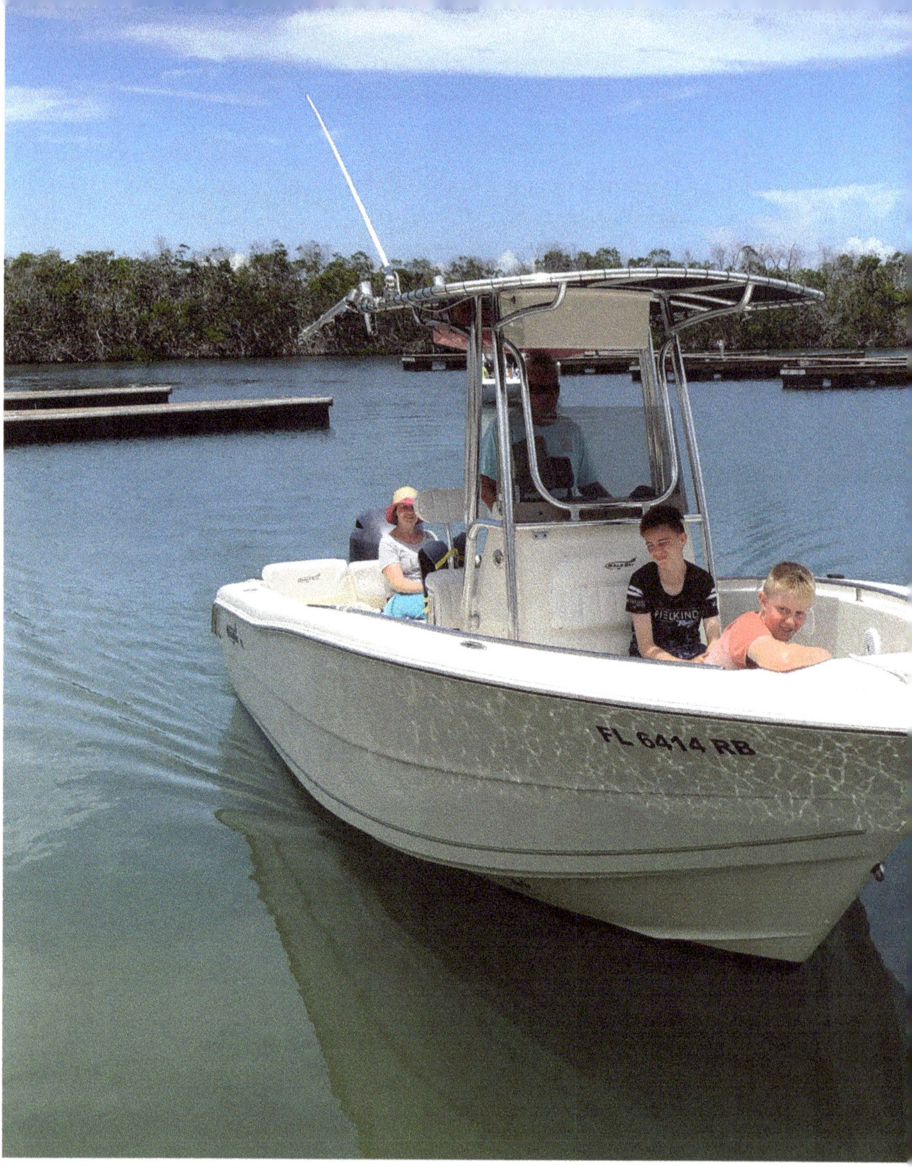

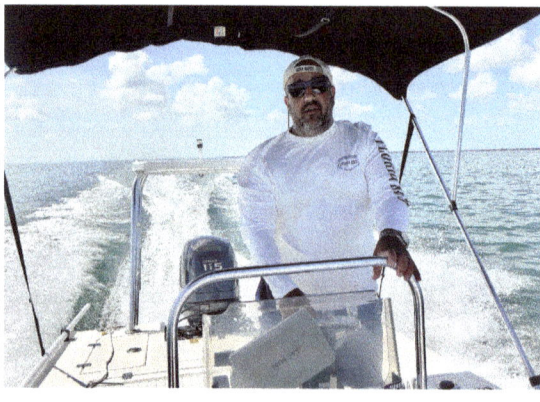

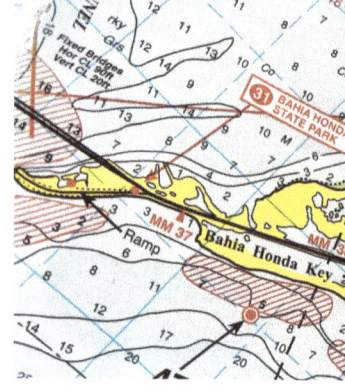

CONTENTS

01 PAGE 1
YOU: STEER IT, ANCHOR IT & DOCK IT
Boating tips and lessons learned
Hands - On

02 PAGE 91
YOU: TRIM IT, TACK IT & SAIL IT
Sailing tips and lessons learned
Hands - On

03 PAGE 113
YOU: RIG IT, BAIT IT & CATCH IT
The how-to of fishing in the Keys
with Captain Jimmy Gagliardini

YOU: STEER IT, ANCHOR IT & DOCK IT

Boating is an activity that comes with many questions. The answers are based on your experience. That is to say, as fun as boating can be, it comes with responsibility. How high is the bridge that you are about to go under? Did you check the chart? Will your mast, T-top and fishing rods clear the overpass? What about at high tide? Is your antenna down? When is low tide? Is the tide incoming or outgoing? What is the depth? Do your passengers get sea sick? What do you do then? What is their swimming ability? Do you have a throw line? How about swim fins? These are all relevant questions for everyday boating. Where can I go? Where can I not go? What should I do if someone falls over? How strong is the current today? How about tomorrow? It changes. Most recreational boaters don't wear a life jacket, but I do recommend that you and your passengers wear a Type 3 PFD, personal flotation device, every time you go boating. Accidents never happen on purpose. I cannot teach you everything in 4-hours time, or even in three 4-hour sessions, but whether one or three lessons, you will know a whole lot more about boating after this hands-on experience than you know now. For many, this is a bucket list lesson. In truth, it should be required.

USEFUL MOBILE APPS

Three crucial pieces of information for boating are weather, wind, and tide. This is where we start. There is a mobile app or website for each category: **MyRadar**, **Windfinder**, and *Tides-4Fishing.com*. Another good app to have on your phone is **Navionics**, a back-up GPS. If your electronics should fail for any reason, or if you get lost while, e.g., kayaking, you have a GPS on your phone. **Fish Rules**, is another very good app – for fish ID, bag limit, and up to date information.

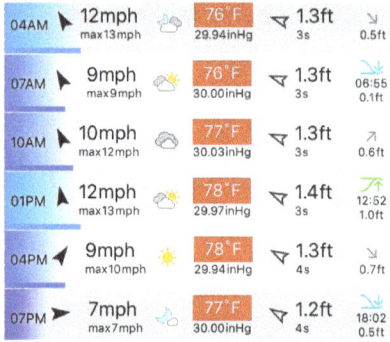

Make sure that your phone is fully charged as part of your checklist routine. Better yet, bring a back-up charging pack with you. Better still, install a USB port on your boat.

SMOOTH SAILING?

Boating doesn't always go smoothly. Sometimes it goes terribly wrong. Remember, every tragic boating incident occurs on a day with best intentions. And, in most cases it could have been avoided. You could have told your only other passenger how to use the radio, start the boat, lift the anchor, and locate the distress gear. You both could have worn life jackets, or not stood up in such a small boat. You should not have brought alcohol with you. You should of had a better appreciation of tide and current. You probably should have waited a bit when you saw those dark skies in the distance. Yes, you had your heart set on boating, and you even made lunch and bought gear. But, those skies – pretty dark, no? And, **Windfinder** called for increased winds. Boating is often a judgment call; err on the side of caution, be smart, go where you know, don't drink and boat. If someone should fall in, be sure to have a plan. If you can't swim, definitely wear a life jacket.

HUMILITY

It is surprising that boaters, unlike automobile drivers, even licensed captains never have to take a car-like road test. No one has to see that you are competent; can dock, anchor, or even understand right of way. To be fair, most boaters are capable. Many boaters know what they are doing, but many do not. On the flip side, some experienced boaters, fishermen and the like, often have a lot more knowledge than a person who just got their captain's license. No newly minted captain wants to admit that they don't know a route, or that they have run aground, but it is often the case. Humility is a huge step in becoming a better boater. Ask questions if you don't know. Practice, pay attention, and practice some more.

Perhaps you decide to save a year or so of guessing and hire a professional charter captain who knows what he or she is doing. You explain to them your wants and needs; local knowledge and safe navigation to a particular location and back. Or, to learn to fish and find a few reliable spots. You want to know what you should have in your tackle box, what bait to use, and how to catch fish, including a few keepers. Is that so much to ask? So, you do. But, you want it to be on your own boat, so to record GPS tracks. It will likely be three to four hours per day, and cost $100+ per hour, but the alternative could translate into years. You don't have years. You want to know now, if only to learn how to operate your new boat better – what hazards to be aware of, and how to properly dock without damaging your boat. You swallow your pride. You hire the right person to teach you: navigation one day, and fishing another. You might hire this person another time or two, or six. It is the best investment one could make. You learn what you need to know, and gain the confidence needed to boat safely. You become intimately acquainted with your area so that your boating days are fun and not stressful. This is retirement time for many, or perhaps – first boat time. How can I enjoy life on the water, you say? That is exactly what we hope to show you.

HANDLING YOUR BOAT

Handling, is in large part what this lesson is all about. In general, people who take our hands-on lesson want to gain confidence in operating their boat beginning with: steering, anchoring, and docking. In addition, they want to know where to go, and how to safely get to a destination. In the Keys, it is the reef and the backcountry. Near you, it is places of interest in a ten-mile radius. We call this your boating playground. In both cases, you want a basic understanding of GPS, so to find and mark good fishing spots and swimming and lobster holes. All that you ask is to get there and back safely.

Because, in boating there are two types of days: those that go well, and those that go wrong. You want it to go well and incident free for a safe return. Does this sound like you?

We will discuss float plan, fuel consumption, and the *what ifs* that could have been prevented, e.g., rather than leave a far away beach a half hour before sunset, maybe better to give yourself an hour. Have a safety plan ready in the event that you break down or run aground. And, bring warm clothes, a towel, water, food, first aid kit, a charged cell phone, marine radio, and some basic tools.

Of course, you have a membership with **Sea Tow** or **TowBoatUS**. Or, Perhaps you have a good insurance policy that includes tow coverage. That, or face the potential of a $1K tow. This is where we begin: checklist preparation – to make sure that we have everything we need. We then leave a dock or boat ramp and discuss different situations such as: accelerating, decelerating, communication, wind and current, turning axis, tilt adjustment, and right of way. Operating a boat is like driving a car x's 1000. It takes lots of time, patience, and practice. Some get it quicker than others. You have to go easy on yourself and take the time you need. You have to trust – and believe.

TRAILERING

Say that you trailer your boat. Is everything secure? If not, that flotation cushion or life jacket could make a pretty nice find for someone along the road. And, if so, you may no longer be compliant with USCG requirements. Did you remember to check that your trailer lights work? Did you forget that you have a trailer attached to your vehicle? It happens. Do you have a strap across the back of the boat or attached to your transom? Is your plug out? How is the air in your tires? Maintenance is a whole other thing. Don't expect trailer brakes to last long – even after a fresh water rinse. Or lights, even though they claim to be submersible, they are not impenetrable. Saltwater and metal are in constant conflict. **Boating Skills and Seamanship** goes into great detail on trailering. What it doesn't tell you is this; don't let anyone distract you while launching or hauling your boat, even officials – they will understand. But, don't take an unnecessary long time in the boat ramp either. Your boat should be ready prior to backing down the ramp. Treat every boating situation as how you would like to be treated. Be mindful – and safe. Figure out a clear communication system for backing your boat down the ramp: car radio off, window down, and you can see one another? You also want to make sure that no one slips on the algae covered ramp at low tide. Perhaps most important, don't get angry with your spouse – No yelling! Did you remember to take the aft strap off the boat, and put the plug in before you launch? Is your vehicle in park, emergency brake on, and motor off before you go behind your boat? Have you seen boat ramp failure videos on YouTube? If not, do so.

PREPARATION MAKES PERFECT

Be sure to leave a float plan with a friend or loved one – tell them where you are going, and what time they should expect you back. Double check your checklist: sunscreen, dive flag, snorkel gear, fishing license, tackle box, rods, bait, credit card, phone, bathing suit, rash guard. Make certain that you have enough fuel – and water. Also, make certain that nothing is hanging overboard that might get damaged, like that $400 rod and reel. Have your dock lines ready and fenders out. Once set, make sure that nothing can fly away, and that everyone is secure. Lines and fenders in. Communicate your intentions, *"Have a seat everyone, I'm about to get on plane. Is everybody ready?" "Ready." "Here we go!"*

THE CHECKLIST

It is important to check your checklist prior to boating. Though, not entirely suited for all, here are a few essentials to think about.

Essentials
- Fuel
- Food
- Water
- Sunscreen
- Phone
- Phone charger
- First aid kit
- GPS
- VHF radio
- Boat registration
- Tools
- Money
- Sunglasses
- Camera
- Binoculars
- Windbreaker
- Bathing suit
- Neck gaiter
- Bandana
- Lip protection
- Boat shoes
- Hat
- Towel
- Change of clothes

Fishing Gear
- Rods
- Tackle box
- Bucket
- Ice
- Pliers
- Rags/gloves
- Aerator
- Fishing license
- Bait
- Regulation book / app
- Filet knife
- Sharpening stone
- Zip-loc bags
- Landing & bait net
- Speargun
- Lobster kit

Snorkel Gear
- Dive flag
- Fins
- Mask
- Snorkel
- Rash guard
- Wetsuit

TWO IS BETTER THAN ONE

It is always better if two people know how to operate the vessel – husband and wife, father and child, couples, friends, etc. Why, might you ask? If anything should happen to the boat operator, and it is not unheard of, the other person might get an opportunity to save a life. Nothing is worse than feeling helpless in a tragic situation. Nothing feels better than saving a life.

USCG REQUIRED EQUIPMENT

The Coast Guard requires specific equipment to be on your boat. They must be USCG approved, accessible, and in serviceable condition. Check for expiration dates.

Have On-Board
- One Type I, II or III life jacket (PFD) for each person on board.
- Lifebuoy or throw cushion
- Fire extinguisher - B -1 type.
- Visual distress signal (flares)
- Sound-producing device (bell, horn, whistle, etc.)
- Vessel lighting
- Ventilation for boats with enclosed engine spaces

THE OUTING

We depart the boat ramp or canal on this beautiful boating day. Our fenders and dock lines are brought in. We reviewed our apps for weather, wind, radar, and tide. We glance at the chart to see the big picture and share it with our passengers – it gains their confidence in you. We make sure that water is pumping through the tracer, so to confirm motor cooling water flow. We take notice of the fuel supply, and also listen to the motor for any anomalies.

We are at idle speed until beyond the shallow water and "no wake" zone. Our bilge pump is on auto. The trim tabs are on. We distribute weight on the boat equally, including our passengers. The motor is all the way down. The GPS is on. So is our sunscreen, visor, and neck gaiter.

We remember to bring a chamois or bandana to wipe dry any unwanted spray off of our polarized sunglasses and GPS. As trivial as it sounds, it is important to have the little things too. We also bring a towel, if only for spray and spills. Everything else – ice, cooler, water, food, bait, fishing license, boat registration, dive flag, and zip ties for the anchor are checked off the checklist. It can be a long list.

We especially make sure to have all of the required USCG equipment: horn, flares, fire extinguisher, not expired or depleted, flotation cushion, a life jacket per person, and original boat registration. We even have a first aid kit, filet knife, and mask and snorkel – just in case anything gets wrapped up in the prop. We let everyone know where this equipment is. We also show them, or at least one person, how to start and stop the boat, anchor location and use, GPS tracks and coordinates, and how to use the marine radio, and if need be – EPIRB. It is the smart thing to do, even if few do it, we do. If alcohol consumption is happening, someone needs to be the designated driver. It too, is the right and legal thing to do.

Off we go. We get on plane toward open water, but soon decide to slow down to idle speed again. There is a small boat anchored near the markers in the shallows. Right of way doesn't always ap-

ply. Instead, we make a judgment call. We call it, common sense. We decide to give way in this situation, and make sure that our boat does not adversely affect theirs. We always have the **4-C** philosophy in play; **caution, common sense, consideration of others,** and **communication**. We don't want to rock the boat, or even make waves. We make sure to communicate effectively – and calmly. We tell our passengers when they can stand, and when they must sit, like a) departing a boat ramp, b) while under way, c) coming into a dock, and d) combining reverse and forward motion. We let our passengers know too, if only our spouse, when we are about to get on plane, and slow down – so not to throw them off balance. We know where we can and cannot go. That is why we looked at the chart. We have the big picture in mind. By the way, there is only one port and one starboard, same as one stern and one bow. It is determined as you are facing the front of the boat or bow (only). Port side is the left side of the boat as you are facing your bow. Port and the word "left" both have four letters. Port, also known as a red wine, is red in navigational lighting terms. Starboard is the right side, and green.

This lesson will help you understand how to: a) operate the vessel in forward and reverse, b) appreciate different conditions, c) get a feel for the boat, and d) give you a better idea of what the right boat is for you. You will learn e) GPS basics, f) proper anchor technique, and retrieving an anchor or stuck anchor without injury to you or your boat. You will also understand g) current and tides, wind and waves, and h) awareness of other boats, buoys, marine life, and debris. The goal is to get you to a point where you can go out, have fun, and return without incident – day in and day out. The hands-on portion of the lesson is soon to begin. I will demonstrate the first exercise and then hand the helm over to you. The first few lessons include communication, getting a feel for the boat, steering, negotiating waves, and overall awareness, including getting up on plane, that :05 to :10 second "take off period" during acceleration where the bows goes up, than comes down, unlike a displacement hull.

THE HANDS-ON PART: HOUR 1

We are in the Gulf side waters off beautiful Bahia Honda Key – or where you live – ready to practice our first hands-on exercise. The helm is yours, not mine. It is now time for you to get your hands on the steering wheel and throttle. Start by feeling the play, if any, in the throttle, that place between forward idle and where it makes the boat go a touch faster. You will both feel it and hear the motor sound change. Often times, there is a good inch of "play" here. Before we get on plane, get a feel for the shifter, and shift between forward and neutral, and neutral and reverse. With today's "digital shifter" or fly-by-wire, it is more sensitive. And, with 300 hp You want to be careful. Gone are the days of, *"Don't grind it – find it!"* Just know that the gear shifter is also the accelerator, so be cautious.

Turn the wheel and take a look back to see what the motor is doing. In many situations, you will turn the motor all the way to one side or the other in neutral, prior to placing the boat into gear. In other instances, like getting on plane, you always look back to make sure that the motor is straight and lowered all the way. And, that there is no play in the accelerator prior to taking off.

You are now ready to get up on plane. As previously mentioned, getting on plane is a gradual yet decisive shift where the bow of the boat climbs up, then lowers. If the passenger load is more than the motor can handle, some aft passengers might have to move to midships as an assist. The bow initially goes up, often to a point where you cannot see over it. Don't fret, it will soon come down, and once it does, you are "on plane". The boat speed increases once you get on plane, so slow down a little, 2 mph, as the bow lowers. You always want to be in control of the boat, not the other way around. Don't slow down so much that your bow starts to rise again. We will operate in the 22 mph range. The boat goes faster, but you don't need to. You need to learn, and focus, and relax. The first exercise is to get on plane a few times so to get a feel for the boat. Next, we will steer the boat in a circle until you cross your own waves. But, don't do too tight a circle. Get a feel for a comfortable turning ratio. It is different in different boats.

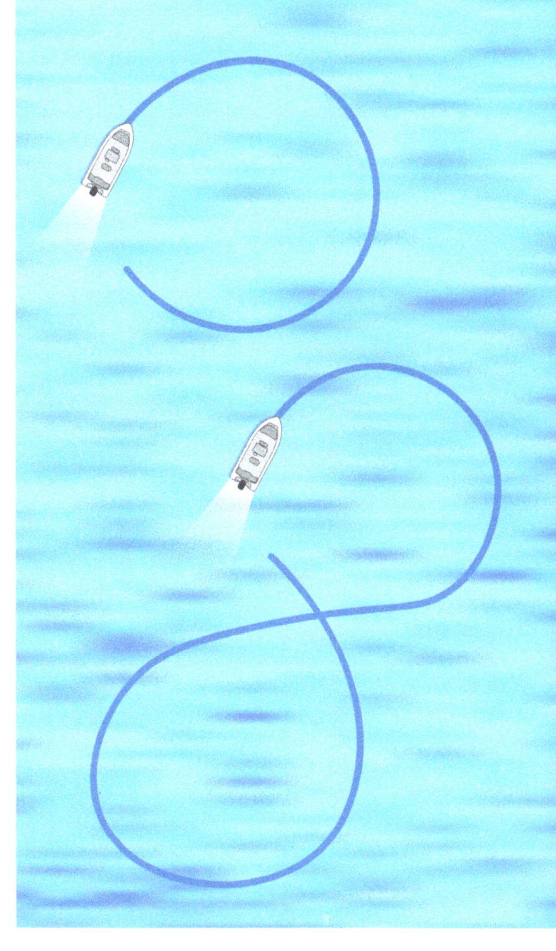

When crossing over waves, slow down right at the wave, comfortably bump over them, then accelerate again. The real practice comes with waves from other boats. What is comfortable passing over waves for the operator, might not be as comfortable for your passengers. We want to transition over waves so that everyone on the boat has a smooth ride. Next, do a circle in the other direction, and then a figure 8. This allows you to get a feel for turning in either direction – where you might need to slow down in the turn, or accelerate, similar to driving a car. This exercise is different in different conditions too, calm waters versus choppy. It is important to practice in both. Let's try that circle again, and a figure 8 in the other direction. Then, more waves and more finesse operating. If you see a boat, safely cross behind it and maneuver in its wake. In boating, you need to multi-task; be aware of your boat, things in the water, and other boats – all at the same time. Let's cross over another wave, but this time do what I call a "hip check." Slow down a tad / two mph just as you get to the wave, while at the same time, turn the boat 90° into the wave so it hits the side or beam of the boat. Afterward, accelerate back up and ride the peaks and valleys of the other boat's wake for a smooth transition. Let's repeat; look around, slow down to a stop, shift between gears, and feel the play in the throttle. Then, look around, get on plane again, and circle to port and starboard. Do a couple of more figure 8's. Get a feel for the turning ratio. Remember to look around whenever you turn or stop. Believe it or not, it takes practice, not unlike taking off and landing.

Let's take a few minutes to study the dash controls, console, and things that we should be aware of on this Bulls Bay 2300 CC boat. All boats are different. Some boats only have a steering wheel or helm, while others have a steering knob in addition to the wheel. This knob with ball bearings makes it possible to steer with one hand, and helps to make turns quicker when the need occurs, like when docking, and only when moving slow vs. fast. The boat has switches too, several of them: accessories, navigation lights, courtesy light, bilge pump, livewell pump, horn, and so forth. There is a stereo, and a USB plug. You can charge your phone here and play music through your phone too. Of course, there is a speedometer, tachometer, and fuel gauge. And, we have a GPS. In addition to chart plotting, I use my GPS for speed, depth, sonar and tide information. The throttle shifter has a button on its side to raise and lower the motor. The "trim tab" buttons balance the boat from side to side. The cabinet above the helm has a VHF radio, first aid kit, binoculars, small tool kit, and a dry box with an air horn, flares, and the boat registration too. We have a T-top, so we attach our life jackets above our heads to have them accessible at all times, as required by law. Our Type B fire extinguisher is attached to the center console and within reach. Our throw cushion is located in an uncluttered hatch, as is our throw line. We make sure to have all of these things at-the-ready.

Our antenna is up and the radio is on channel 16 whenever we are underway. The cushions are snapped in because we don't want to

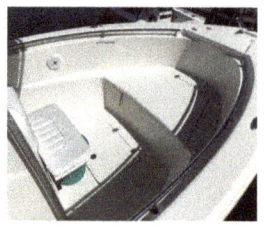

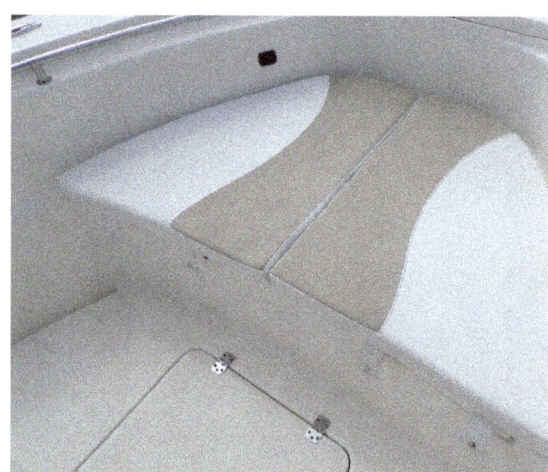

Clockwise: Stern cushions, bow cushions; Center console with helm and controls, leaning post; Stern: battery box, livewell storage, Bow: anchor locker, bow storage, seat, bilge access

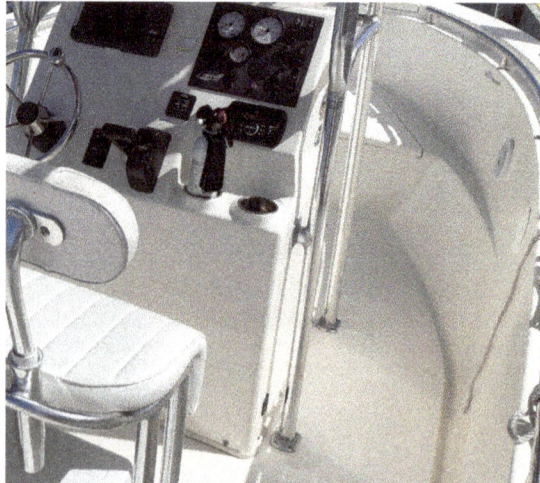

lose these relatively expensive items. The transom well in the back of the boat (stern) has a wash down hose controlled by the accessory switch. There is a hatch too, where if opened, we see a bilge pump, livewell pump, and wash down pump – the pump for the deck hose – in the bilge. The three hatches beneath the rear seats include, from starboard to port, the battery box and main power switch, the livewell, and a small compartment for storage. In the front of the boat (bow) is an anchor locker with a Danforth anchor. But, we also have a plow anchor in a basket with 200' of line (rode), and 5' of 3/8" chain. We have dry storage compartments beneath the forward seat, and inside of the center console too. There is also a floor hatch, where we sometimes keep an extra bucket. We store our drinks cooler beneath the leaning post seat. Know where everything is, and stow your gear accordingly. It all needs to be accessible and shipshape.

It is now time to maneuver through the many lobster pots near the bridge and to the bridge itself. It is helpful to know whether the tide is incoming or outgoing here. The lobster traps and buoys have a long line between them. You don't want to run over the line. It can result in a lost trap for the lobsterman, and getting the line wrapped around your prop – another reason to keep a serrated knife vs. filet knife, in this case, on board. When in doubt, pass the buoy on the downwind side. You will now set a course in-between the buoys, all the while finding a spot on the horizon, or perhaps the center of the bridge itself to steer toward. It is important to have an object or compass bearing to steer toward for a consistent track. If you don't, and you are traveling a long distance, it could prove inefficient. Once near the bridge, look for other boats and hazards. Pick a spot between the pilings to drive under the bridge. Once through to the other side, take another quick look around. Then, slow down to idle speed, and neutral. Everything on a boat, steering and throttle, is done in small increments. You don't want to throw anyone off balance, so you operate in a smooth and subtle manner. See how much you have accomplished already? You have even crossed from one major body of water, the Gulf or bay side to the ocean side, or the Florida Straits. For others, it could be starting in one bay, and navigating around a lighthouse hazard to another bay, like in Douglaston, NY on the Long Island Sound. Or, where you live. And, this all takes place in the very first hour.

HANDS-ON HOUR 2

Next, we'll pull into a marina and observe the "no wake" zone. It is always surprising to guess what no wake is without looking back at your motor, especially if the wind is behind you. Many people slow down to a slow speed when passing another boat, but not to a "no wake" speed. No wake generally means the slowest speed that your boat can go in forward – where you don't make waves. Medium forward speed puts off a sizable wake, more than you think, so dial it back to forward idle. Now, when current and wind start to affect your boat, you will need to increase to "steerage" speed, or a tad more, so that you have control of the boat. There are times when you have to tell the boat what to do, not ask it. But, you also have to be observant and considerate of other boaters. A good exercise for telling the boat what to do happens during a 3-point turn, especially when wind is a factor. You are going to turn the boat 180°. In neutral, turn the wheel all the way to port. Shift into forward and begin your turn. As the bow of your boat comes toward 90°, you have momentum. Now, shift into neutral and steer all the way to starboard. Only then, do you go reverse, until near 180°, then neutral, forward and neutral. What we have done here, is put on the brakes. But, the boat will tend to slide in the direction of the original turn. *Note: You never want to shift straight from reverse to forward, or vice versa. You want to use neutral to protect the motor.*

If it is a tad windy while attempting a 3-point turn, you will have to tell the boat what to do, meaning that you will make the motor growl or thrust a tad, but without throwing anyone off balance. Communicate to your passengers, *"Could everyone please sit down for a minute This maneuver can throw you off balance."* Now, turn the wheel all the way to starboard, and this time shift forward – but with

a little growl added to it. Listen to it, *Grrr!* As you see the bow commit toward 90°, go to neutral and then (in neutral) turn to all the way to port. Reverse with a *Grrr!* to 180°, then neutral. *BTW: I explain twin motor operation a little later with an illustrated diagram (see pages 44 - 45).*

The 3-point turn is often used when positioning yourself to a boat ramp, when docking, and when turning around in a tight space. The more narrow the area, and the more windy, the higher degree of difficulty. It is very important to keep conscious of your sideway momentum, and the other boats around you. Always prepare to fend off, but hope not to. You never want hit another boat. And, if necessary, you only want to fend off at the slowest speed possible. You could get hurt otherwise. When docking, combine these same elements of finesse operation, i.e., forward then neutral, turn when you are one boat length away from the dock, forward, until approximately 20° off parallel, neutral, quickly turn the motor all the way toward the dock (if counter intuitive), then reverse, and neutral.

Let's get back on the water and see what the current is doing. It is actually difficult to see current with the naked eye unless you are near a bridge piling or a buoy. Current is something that you feel when swimming – more than see. There can be little or no current one minute, and then strong current 5-minutes later. It is why I recommend to always wear fins when swimming. Tide and current go hand in hand, so another good reason to understand tidal coefficient, or the amount of water movement from one tide to another.

Let's practice anchoring in current, and communication between the captain and first mate. Important information to remember when anchoring is the following: know whether it is an incoming, outgoing, or slack tide. Feel where the wind is coming from. Look around for other anchored vessels, and the direction in which their boat is pointing. Also, look to see if there is a buoy of some sort nearby. If you see a boat at anchor, you want to point in the direction that they are pointing. This means, position your boat in said direction prior to lowering your anchor. The "buoy of some sort" will later act as a distance indicator to let you know if your anchor is dragging or not. Look over to it from time to time. Select your anchor location, and give yourself room, so in the event that you do break loose, you will not hit anything, e.g., the bridge or another boat. The person at the helm and the person at the anchor need to communicate with one another. *Note: When on a boat, if you want a person to hear what you are saying, your mouth should be facing in their direction.* It helps to speak-up too. We will also practice hand signal communication.

The helmsperson will position the boat into the current until you are ready with the anchor. The helmsperson will also factor in the depth. Once forward momentum stops, lower the anchor down at the helmsperson's command. Do not throw the anchor, lower it.

Then, after the chain, let go until the anchor hits bottom. At this point, the helmsperson will go a tad reverse, then neutral, so to gain backward momentum, This action also causes the anchor to lay down. In other cases, a strong current alone can draw you back. It is important that the anchor person has good footing and balance.

The anchor person lets out a guesstimate amount of rode while the boat is in reverse. Your arms wing span is your approximate height. If 10' depth, let out 6 to 8 wing span lengths, or 50'. You will do a 5:1 ratio count of depth to scope before taking a 360° "wrap" or "bight" around the cleat. If more current, let more line out. You can now tie your cleat knot. Make sure that the anchor has a secure hold before turning the motor off. Give the line a tug and make sure that the boat is pointed toward the anchor. Only then are you "set." We will get into specifics on the water, including retrieving a deep anchor, getting a stuck anchor out, and working together to retrieve an anchor in current. Let's enjoy the surroundings for a minute before moving onto the next exercise. If your boat is laying sideways to the anchor, you are either dragging or it is slack tide, that short period of time when the tide is neither coming in or going out.

I use a technique once anchored, where I disengage the kill switch, the plastic shim attached to the key. The motor will not run without the shim being engaged. By disengaging it, I am reminded to bring the ladder in, and the dive flag down. It is a very good habit to get into. It should be noted that this "kill switch" is intended to be hooked to the operator of the vessel, you, in the event that the operator is somehow tossed from the boat. Once the operator is pulled far enough from the helm, the kill switch will disengage, and the boat motor stops. That is the theory anyway. Few people use it this way because many operators are only wearing a bathing suit and there is nothing to attach it to. You need to figure out a convenient method to attach the tether to your body so to have room to move while at the same time, the kill switch can do its job. I personally feel that the kill switch shim should be independent of the key chain, and that the hook, or connection to the boat operator should be more secure than a belt loop. A wrist D-ring is a great safety concept that can save a life. The connection is: a) independent of the key, b) less confining, and c) stronger. No matter what the operator is wearing (or not), the wrist D-ring bracelet with lanyard and shim is a great solution.

Retrieving an anchor can present different set of challenges: rocks, wind, current, nearby hazard, deep depth, or a combination of these. For a normal 10' depth retrieval, you can simply: a) bring the ladder in, b) take the dive flag down, c) engage the kill switch, d) start the motor, e) look around for other boats and waves, and then, f) at the helmsperson's command, bring the anchor in. Remember, you always want to have the motor started before you pull up the anchor. You also keep the motor running until the anchor is set. You will un-cleat the rode or line before you start to pull the anchor up.

If the anchor feels too heavy due to current, you and the helmsperson can work together to make it easier. This is achieved with hand signals. A karate chop hand signal in the direction of the anchor, means go forward in this direction. A fist means to shift into neutral. The anchor person is looking at the anchor. The person at the helm is watching your hand signals, and is otherwise aware of his or her surroundings. As the retrieval happens, the anchor person will "bird nest" the anchor rode into the anchor locker or basket. This means that the line goes back in as it came out – naturally, never coiled first. When the anchor person sees the chain, he/she makes a fist, then carefully brings the chain over the gunwale so not to scratch or damage the boat. You also want to make sure to clean off any mud or seagrass before lifting the anchor over the gunwale. And, remember to replace the plastic zip tie immediately if it is broken (discussed later). You always want a ready anchor. The very end of the 200' anchor rode, aka the bitter end, is usually attached to the boat with a bowline knot. *Note: When current is especially strong near a bridge, especially when boating alone, an anchor buoy kit, normally used for deep water retrieval, is a great tool to hoist your anchor to get away from the bridge safely.* Let's demonstrate this.

Say that you are by yourself at a bridge and the current is whipping through at 3 to 5 knots, too strong for you to safely pull the anchor up by yourself. We have a solution. The deep anchor / strong current retrieval kit consists of a locking stainless steel ring, 5' of line, and an 18" round buoy. Simply place the open ring around the anchor rode just outside of your boat – and lock the ring. Once secure, toss the buoy into the water. Make certain that your fishing lines are in, and that one side of your gunwale is clear – no rods in rod holders, and keep passengers clear too. You are going to drive forward, 30° off the anchor – to the side that the anchor line is over the bow, port or starboard. You can move the anchor line to one guide or the other if need be. Drive forward at 3 - 5 knots and 30° off your anchor. *Note: The goal is to drive past your anchor to pull it out.*

Aside from retrieving your anchor, and/or to get away from a hazard, you need to make sure that the anchor rode does not get caught in your propeller. Turn 20° away from the anchor, and go only 3 - 5 mph, as you keep the rode away from the prop. You are only driving for twice the length of the anchor depth, or far enough to where you feel safe, e.g., from a bridge. The forward motion makes

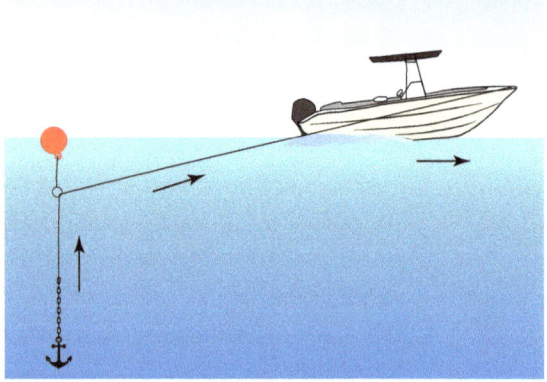

the ring slide down the rope. The buoy goes underwater forcing the anchor to come up. Once you have gone a hundred or so feet, the anchor is magically in the ring just below the surface. Now, all you need to do is turn sideways to the anchor, and pull the anchor rode into the boat until you get to the anchor. This simple yet very effective anchor retrieval kit was designed for deep anchor haul out, but it is great too for solo boaters in strong current near a bridge.

Let's take a minute to discuss the different design parts of a boat: bow, stern, transom, bottom, chine, waterline, freeboard, gunwale, deck, center console, T-top, etc. *See diagram.* It is confusing to be sure, deciding what boat to get, and what questions you should ask about power and your motor. I will try to demystify it here. You don't necessarily have to start with a 16' boat and work your way up to a 26' boat. You can pretty much learn on any size boat, but I do recommend starting in the 23' range like the one I have. This Bulls Bay has a high freeboard (water to gunwale distance), because it is designed for offshore seas – to keep dry. The length is manageable though it is affected by wind more than a boat closer to the water. A boat just 2' longer spans waves better for a more comfortable ride in choppy conditions. Then again, a 28' to 30' boat is a lot more boat and cost, and a little more difficult to tow, launch, and dock. A longer boat often has more power, two outboards, so more maintenance too. The wider the boat, the more stable. This 23' boat with its 8' beam is fairly stable. A strong transom is vital because the motor is heavy and provides lots of torque. The gunwale ties together the sides of the boat with the bow and stern. If you enjoy fishing, it is convenient to have several rod holders in your gunwale, perhaps four or more on each side. A convenient livewell location is a big consideration for fishing too. Granted, any bait livewell is a good one, but location matters, so if located under the seat, don't forget to re-attach those pricey seat cushions afterward.

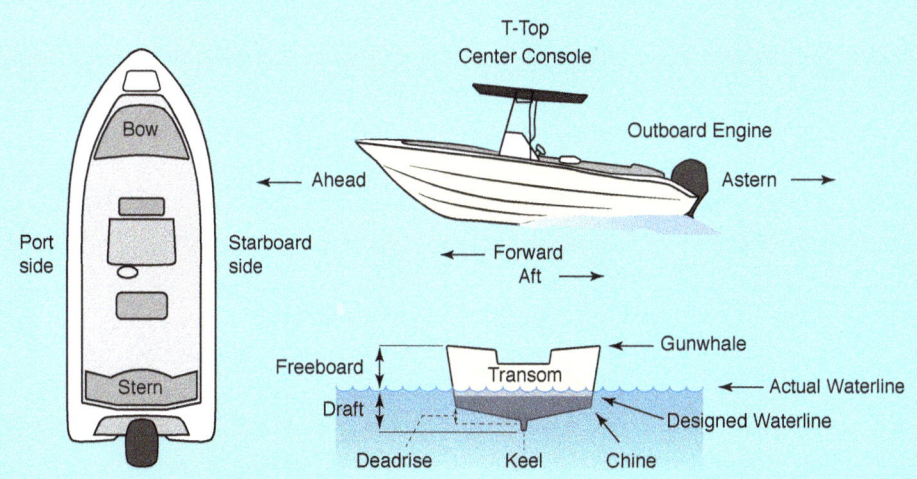

The most common all-around boat for the Keys, and pretty much everywhere these days, is a center console with an outboard motor. Center consoles are easy to steer, easy to anchor, and easy to dock. Boats can be expensive, and are. That said, you get what you pay for. If you compare a brand new $70K boat to a brand new $170K boat, the differences are many. The less expensive boat might have been assembled more haphazardly, meaning that the wiring to the console might need to be upgraded. There might also be some other cheap parts, and weak spots in the fiberglass that will reveal stress cracks over time and need repair. This is especially true if you make too many hard landings. The T-top on a less expensive boat is canvas, while the more expensive boat is a hard top. The more expensive boat has lots of rod holders, while the less expensive boat has perhaps only two. The livewell location is better thought out on the more expensive boat. And, there are more bells and whistles as well: outriggers, GPS, a better stereo, and maybe even a head / toilet. As for power, most all brands: Yamaha, Mercury, and Suzuki are go-to dependable outboards. Get the one with the best price, warranty, and the one most convenient to be serviced by an authorized mechanic near you. I recommend too, that you consider powering your boat with the maximum power that the boat is rated for. But, research the cost and technical pros and cons. If it's just going to be two of you, a boat that is paired with a 200 hp should be plenty. If for a family of four or more, maybe a 300 hp is better. Another consideration is what you can afford. Case in point, I opted for the 300 hp / $70K boat and did some upgrades.

Your boat will come with a stainless steel or aluminum prop, but is it the right prop? What is the right prop? And, how do you know?

 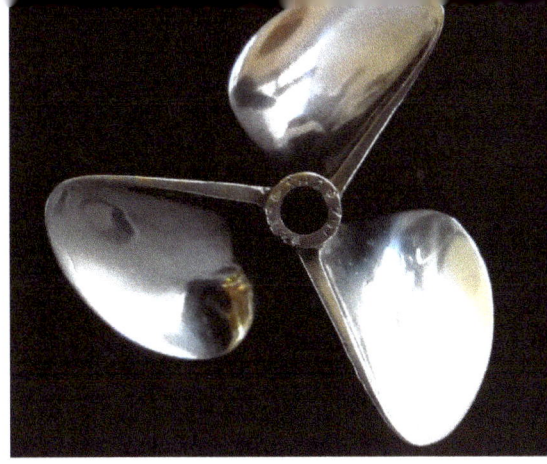

There is a basic formula that calculates speed, tachometer and your motor in relationship to the boat, passenger load, and prop diameter and pitch. All boats are different. Even the same motor, e.g., 200 Yamaha four stroke, might need a different prop depending on the boat it is on. It is best understood with a prop specialist, like Prop Tech of Marathon, FL. They will have you run your boat wide open with two or three passengers and ask you to take note of your speed and tachometer RPM's. Also, make sure that your cavitation plate on the motor is level with your boat bottom. There is a magic number that you hope to achieve for maximum efficiency, like 40 mph and 5800 RPM, but this is just an example. This overlooked aspect of testing a new boat and motor might otherwise demand a new $600 prop purchase. It is just one reason that you do a sea trial and have a prop specialist help you before you buy. I had a three blade 15" diameter x 21" pitch RH prop on my motor but it wasn't turning enough RPM's. A 14¾" diameter and 15" pitch with a four blade prop made a world of difference in: plane pick-up, smoother ride, speed, and a 700 RPM tach increase to 5800 from 5100. I changed the hub too, to silence a chatter noise. So, don't discount the value of a right prop.

A center console boat, with a good outboard and T-top for shade is a great all-around boat. You can cruise, snorkel, fish, and play with tow toys. It is an ideal boat for both charter and recreational uses. If you normally go out with two people, a 23' boat offers plenty of space – up to six passengers. If you trailer your boat, you don't need bottom paint. If you keep it in the water for the season, you might want a good bottom paint job. That is, unless you are in a slip and can take the boat out every two weeks to power wash it. Then, don't. Maintain your boat regularly and keep a maintenance log.

Count down from 100 hours (each time you go out) to record hours for oil change. Also, take note of your boat and motor serial numbers, spark plug type, fuel water separator and all of the parts your boat requires for 100 hour service. My 300 hp Yamaha requires that my oil, oil filter, lower unit lube, spark plugs, fuel water separator, in-line fuel filter, and impeller all need to be changed every 100 hours. Thermostats, and internal and external anodes need to be change every year. It is advised to do a fresh water motor rinse after every outing. If you take very good care of your boat, your boat will take very good care of you. One more thing, tell your passengers to take their shoes off and to wipe their feet, before coming aboard your new boat.

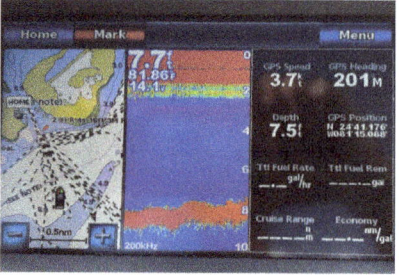

OK, lets take a look at the GPS for speed, depth, compass direction, shoals versus islands, hazards and markers, tracks and routes, and tides. That is pretty much all you will ever need to know. But, first – hydrate. It is super important to drink fluids and apply sunscreen wherever you boat, even if it is overcast. Salt dehydrates. And, when boating here in the Keys, please consider reef safe sunscreen.

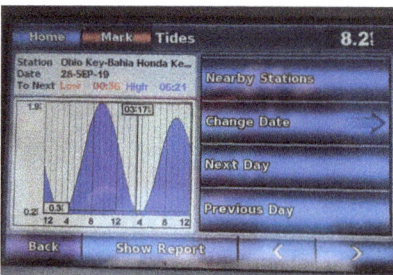

The GPS shows chart, tracks, sonar, speed, depth, direction, position and tides

This is the plan, we will navigate around a sandbar hazard, and pass through the narrow channel marked by PVC pipes. Then, it's off to the backcountry and around No Name Key. Or, we might circle around from the Gulf side to the ocean side and steer along contour lines, depth changes, and back to where we started. In either situation, we will anchor again, but reverse roles of helmsperson and anchor person. The decision to head north toward the backcountry, or south into the ocean is generally a judgment call based on wind and comfort. If the wind is blowing from the south and east, we might decide to go north and west. Why get beat up and wet if you don't have to? It is one of the great advantages of having two unique bodies of water in your boating playground. You have a choice to stay comfortable versus get beat up. Then again, some days are not good boating days – so you don't.

HANDS-ON HOUR 3

Contours lines or no, and Gulf side versus the Atlantic side, or Florida Straits, we practice the same exercise; watch for other boaters and marine life, go where the GPS says we can, keep on the side of caution, use common sense, be considerate and communicate – the **4-C's**, your boating mantra for an enjoyable day on the water. Once around a sandbar hazard, and through the narrow man made channel where we may or may not have to slow to idle speed for snorkelers, we proceed to the next channel. If you look down at your hand as if admiring a ring, your fingers represent mangrove islands, and in between, are the channels of water. It is the same with our "groove and spur" barrier reef four miles out to sea, the third largest barrier reef in the world, in that your fingers represent coral, and in between, are sand channels.

Learning is not experiencing when all things go right. Like life, you often learn when things go wrong. It is why we practice potential run-aground situations, to pay attention. In fact, paying constant attention takes time, but you must. We will get up on plane and practice using the trim tabs for port and starboard balance. The trim tabs are often used to raise the weather side of the boat to keep passengers dry. It is also used to counter weight imbalance: a 250 lb person on the port side, versus an 80 lb person on the starboard side.

The motor trim, on the other hand, raises and lowers the bow to a degree. It is also used to raise the motor as needed; hauling your vessel, and operating in shallow water are but two instances.

It is not just important to know what the tide is where you are, but also to know what the tide is doing where you are going. And, whether a king tide or minus tide is in the mix. And, what might the coefficient be, together with wind direction. Not necessarily related but important nonetheless: you never want to unintentionally run aground, especially during an outgoing tide, or while going fast. The experience can be long and cold – possibly even life threatening. Know your tides, and the tide flow direction. If it is an incoming tide, it is safer to carefully "beach" your boat intentionally. If in the opposite scenario, and you beach your boat on an outgoing tide, you'll want to drop an anchor in 3' to 4' depth so to pull yourself out. Otherwise, be observant. But, tide is different in different scenarios, e.g., it can be high tide at US 1 on Big Pine Key, and low tide at No Name Key (in the very same channel, at the very same time, just two miles apart). This is due to two separate bodies of water and opposite tide flows. The next week, the tides of these two locations can be the same, both high or low at the same time. Use the microphone on your phone to command – e.g., *Tides4Fishing.com / Spanish Harbor vs. Tides4Fishing.com / Bogie Channel* to check. Which reminds me, let's go to our GPS and check the tides. Let's also go to our apps and see what **MyRadar** and **Windfinder** say. A visual look-see is always a good idea too. The meteorologist said there was a 30% chance of rain today, but where? Storms are often very isolated in the Keys. If you see a downpour in one direction, go in the direction of blue skies and resume your day. Conversely, if you find yourself about to be caught in a downpour, head in. If extreme, prepare to lower the anchor with a 8:1 ratio, and wait it out. Though it doesn't seem so, it is sure to pass and be super calm afterward. But, sometimes predictions are inaccurate, and a light breeze can turn into a 40 mph squall. What if something goes wrong, as in – really wrong? Remember your PFD? That in mind, let's review a man overboard scenario. It is a drill that few boaters ever practice. But, you should, because it can mean the difference between life and death.

MAN OVERBOARD? NEVER

Man or person goes overboard. What do you do? The scenarios are many: alone, with others, moving boat, anchored boat, medical emergency, something silly? You never know. Do you have any idea what you would do in a real life scenario other than panic? Few do. Your life jackets are very accessible, or should be (by law). *Note: This is where you wish that you had gotten into the everyday habit of wearing a PFD, and have everyone on your boat wear a simple lightweight Type 3 PFD, personal flotation device.* In the eyes of USCG, the Type 3 PFD counts as a life jacket, only if you are wearing it. And, in a situation such as this – it makes a world of difference. You never know when tragedy will strike. It will always take you by surprise. That, I can guarantee. Best to be prepared.

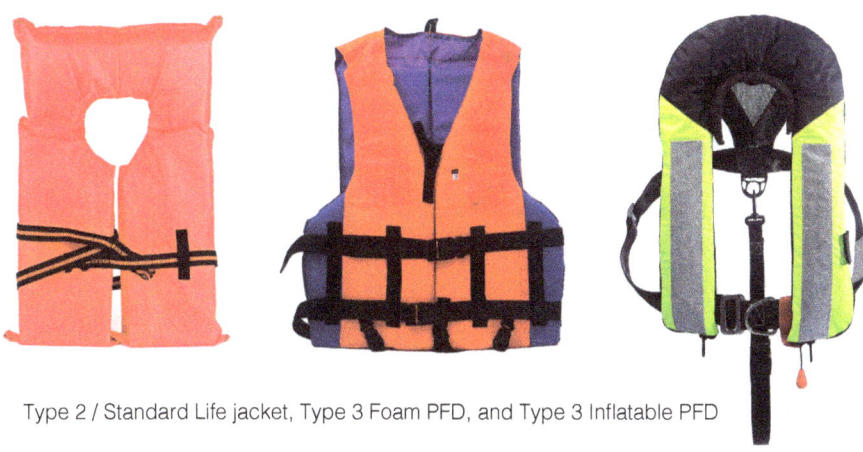

Type 2 / Standard Life jacket, Type 3 Foam PFD, and Type 3 Inflatable PFD

But, the reality is this, most people don't wear a life jacket, so I don't depict that image in this book. I would like to show every person in the photos of this book wearing a life jacket, but that is not a real life scenario in everyday boating – so I do not. I cannot play pretend. I can only recommend that you at least consider a Type 3 PFD, especially if out alone, or out as a couple. It can save a life, and does.

Back to the man overboard: You have a throw cushion. Practice throwing it. You might have a throw line with a fender buoy attached, even better. Is there current? You DO NOT want to dive in after the man overboard. Drowning people tend to fight for higher ground, you, in which case you could both drown. Try to find a solution. Is the victim alert, conscious, startled, injured? Are you at anchor? It's a good thing that you learned how to start the motor if need be. Do you have some rope, or the slightest idea how to tie a knot? Do you know anything about CPR? Did you bring your first aid kit? Is your phone handy? How about your marine radio? Are other boaters nearby who you can get assistance from? Maybe the horn is best. This is panic mode, where many peoples reaction freeze, but you have to remain calm. You rehearsed this. You can do it – save your loved one. How do you get him or her: secure, on board, rescued at least? Think what you might do next time if this scenario were to ever present itself. I am talking about being ready, prepared, and having the tools and a plan ready for such a scenario. Knowing your options is a whole lot better than not. Let's demonstrate one such possibility, and practice marine radio, horn, and rope toss = options.

If you or a passenger goes overboard, do your best not to panic. Instead, remember what you practiced. If you are the victim, try to maintain calm. If anything, swim perpendicular to the current, to more shallow water. Repeat: If a person falls in, it is tempting but potentially twice as dangerous for another person to jump in after them. Remember the flotation cushion? Now is the time to use it. Better yet, have a 50' line with a buoy or life ring tied to it. Toss that to your man overboard. Is there another boat nearby? If you feel that the person's life is in danger, and a boat is nearby, use the horn (five short blasts). It's a good thing that you practiced this. It is good too, that you are comfortable with the VHF radio. And, that you know how to find your GPS latitude and longitude coordinates.

Use the VHF radio if need be, and call for help on channel 16. But, try your cell phone first. The three types of distress calls on the radio are **MAYDAY = imminent danger to life**; **Pan-Pan, Pan-Pan, Pan-Pan,** pronounced *"Pahn-Pahn"* **= announces an urgent message**, a request for assistance if a boat or its crew is in danger, but the situation is not life threatening. And, **Sécurité, Sécurité, Sécurité = notice to other boaters** regarding, e.g., a navigational hazard, or intention of a large vessel to get underway.

Another option for a distress call includes pairing your GPS with your VHF, the DSC system via your TowBoatUS membership. Or, if you have an EPIRB on board where alert to the USCG happens with the simple push of a distress button, now might be the time to use it. Then again, it might be a simple as using your air horn to a passing boater. The important thing is, know what to do in a life threatening situation. And, know how to communicate on your VHF.

MV Lucky Me: *Mayday, Mayday, Mayday. This is the motor vessel Lucky Me, can anyone hear me?*

Mayday, Mayday, Mayday. This is the motor vessel Lucky Me, can anyone hear me? – over

Stop and listen for a response, then:

USCG:
Motor vessel Lucky Me, this is USCG sector Key West. Switch and call on channel 22.

MV Lucky Me:
Roger, switching to 22. USCG, this is the motor vessel Lucky Me. – over

USCG:
Go ahead motor vessel Lucky Me.

MV Lucky Me:
My husband fell overboard and we need help. I was able to throw a tow line to him, but I think he hurt his shoulder and I can't lift him. What should I do? – over

USCG:
USCG to motor vessel Lucky Me. See if you can get him to the boat, and secure him with a rope around his torso to a cleat. – over

The USCG will ask you to describe your boat, the name of your vessel, whether you are at anchor or adrift. They will want your coordinates so to immediately get someone headed to your location. Many people don't know what to do in the given situation. That is why it is so important to practice this very real life threatening scenario. People think that a life or death situation will never happen to them – until, it does.

> **MV Lucky Me:**
> Copy that. We are a 23' long, white vessel with a T-top. We are approximately 3 miles south of Little Palm Island. We are 2 adults and 2 children. – over
>
> **USCG:**
> Roger, white vessel with T-top. 2 adults and 2 children, 3 miles south of Little Palm Island. Your coordinates? – over
>
> **MV Lucky Me:**
> Our latitude and longitude position is ... and ... We are at anchor. Please come soon. – over
>
> **USCG:**
> Copy, motor vessel Lucky Me. We have someone headed to your location. If you see a passing boat, use your horn– over
>
> **MV Lucky Me;**
> Thank you, Coast Guard, I will – over
>
> **USCG:**
> USCG, out. Switching and standing by on Channel 16.
>
> **MV Lucky Me;**
> Switching and standing by on channel 16. Motor Vessel Lucky Me, over and out.

You do what you can to keep yourself and your children / other passengers calm. You get a rope and wrap it around the man overboard torso and armpits, then back to a cleat on the boat. Perhaps you can get a life jacket over his neck, if only to keep his head above water. Wait for the Coast Guard, but have a horn ready to signal a passing boat too, (5 blasts and wave arms) for assistance.

Every situation is different, but in every case it is best to be at anchor and stay where the man overboard took place so to lock in your coordinates for rescue. There is of course the issue of getting an exhausted man into the boat. You may or may not get him in the boat, but at least you kept his / her head above water and saved a loved one. The hope is that this drill gives you a better appreciation for what can (and does) happen when you least expect it – a relaxing vacation in the FL Keys, or anywhere greeted with tragedy. You have to be prepared and ready – knowledge of rescue gear, its location, and also psychologically prepare too, if only in the back of your mind.

WHAT IF YOU HEAR A MAYDAY CALL?

In the event that you hear a MAYDAY call over the radio, your first instinct should be to grab your cell phone and bring up a note app. Write down all information: boat name, description, location, situation, etc. This is very important. You might be able to save a life. If the Coast Guard doesn't answer the distress call within two minutes, call the USCG on channel 16 and repeat the distress message, stating clearly that you are relaying the message. Stand by on channel 16 to follow any USCG instructions. If you are fishing alone, it is important that you wear a PFD at all times. Many of us don't take man overboard drills as serious as we should. It could even be 90% of us. We don't wear a PFD when we should. We don't have a life line or Type IV throwable cushion ready. Only 10% of boats are connected to a DSC system. In this case, one push of a button could save your life. In most every case, time is not on your side.

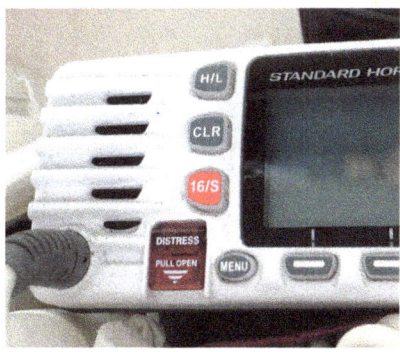

The DSC (digital selective calling) maritime distress and safety call system allows VHF radios to send an automated mayday that alerts the U.S. Coast Guard.

It is not unheard of to fall overboard when out alone. It can happen, and does, even to the most experienced boater. It is not uncommon for someone to fall in during a strong current. And, you're not wearing a PFD, or fins. And, the light is fading – as is your strength. Standard boating safety measures should not be taken lightly. You and at least one other person on board should know the location of the throw line, cushion, flares, horn, and fire extinguisher. One other person should know how to start the motor, lift the anchor, use the radio, and operate the boat. CPR and knot tying is a bonus.

HANDS-ON HOUR 4

We chose the backcountry and the direction of the No Name bridge. But first, let's cut over to the right, or to starboard. Did you look over your shoulder before you turned? You would have if you were in a car. Keep going straight ahead for a little bit, halfway between here and the bridge. Now, stop! Did you look behind you to see if another boat was there or did you just react to my command? Always look first. Besides, you were just about to ride onto some very shallow grass, and it's a falling tide. You should have looked at your GPS and questioned me. Okay, now let's raise the motor so not to damage the sea floor. Lets leave this area at the slowest possible speed until we are in 4' of water. Next, lower the motor all the way. Look around you. Communicate to your passengers, *"Is everybody ready?"* And, get on plane toward the bridge.

Let's talk about the things that we should consider around a bridge. There is current, incoming or outgoing tide, and potential shelter from a passing storm. There is the height of the bridge, and the lights. What do the lights represent? It is the channel. It is also

a no fishing zone. Up above are signs located to either side of the channel declaring a "no fishing" zone. People rarely fish in between the signs, but not never. The only never is this – You never want to get caught by a fish hook while passing under a bridge in a boat. So, go slow, be observant, and proceed through. Another good reason to go slow is the narrow space framed out by very hard concrete pilings. What if your steering were to fail at this moment? It has happened.

Let's reverse roles in anchoring once again. Survey the area, other boats, wind and current, and work together. Look for other anchored boats, and their bow direction. Know what the tide is doing, incoming or outgoing. Be sure to anchor outside of the channel. The GPS informs us of our depth. You know all of this. The anchor is ready. The boats forward motion has stopped. Lower the anchor, and after the chain, let it go. The helmsperson goes into reverse, then neutral. The anchor person counts off wingspan scope length for a 5:1 ratio based on depth. He / she then takes a wrap around the cleat, before locking it off. The anchor sets, and the bow is facing the anchor. If to snorkel or swim, and if shallow enough, go to the anchor to make sure of its hold so to insure that the boat will not brake free and drift away while you are in the water.

We can go back the way we came, or we can circumnavigate No Name Key. Let's go around the island. The GPS tells us that there is some shallow water off the tip of the island, a teardrop of sorts. It is a shoal or shallow area created by current over time. It is clearly marked on both the chart and the GPS. This is common to all islands, shoals created from current sediment over time. Look at the GPS and tell me where you can and cannot go. Take wind and tide into consideration too, and discuss what track will keep us most protected. Also, decide which side of the boat to raise, if only a tad, due to wind and spray. Trim tabs often need a reset.

RIGHT OF WAY

See that boat coming toward us? It is time to practice right of way and rules of the road; when we are the stand-on vessel or the give-way vessel. There is right of way in boating, similar to cars. We stay to the right and pass, in most cases, left to left or port to port.

There are definite rules of the road, but common sense plays the biggest role – avoid accidents and confrontation whenever possible. In short, the boat on the right has the right of way. Rather than linger in a head-on scenario, move to your right or starboard. If it is going to take you considerably off course and there is plenty of room, it is permissible to go to port instead. The most important thing is to let the other boat know your intention. Practice good seamanship, keep a good lookout, and maintain safe speed and distance. There are a few markers on our way back to the marina. Let's stop and review them. You don't learn by zooming by. You learn by referencing it with your GPS. Remember to look first before you turn or stop.

Let's quickly review vessels that have right of way over others. Power vessels must give way to those: not under command (anchored and disabled vessels), restricted in ability to maneuver (being towed, towing), constrained by draft, engaged in fishing, sailboat under sail, and when overtaking a vessel from behind. Use your reference book; **Boating Skills and Seamanship**, for rules, marker type, and technical information.

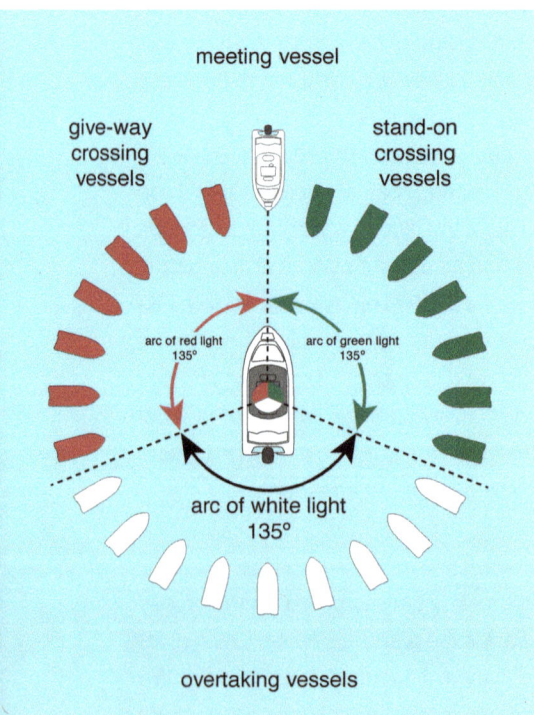

At night, it is important to understand lights; **red = port, green = starboard, white = stern or masthead**. White is an anchor light when side lights are extinguished. **Red and white = you must give way**. Slow down and allow other vessel to pass, or turn to right and pass behind other vessel. **White light = is a stand on vessel**, either under way or anchored. You may pass on either side. **Green and white light = you are the stand on vessel** but remain vigilant and steer clear. If it is just a red light or a green light, you are most likely encountering a sail boat underway. Give way. It is smart to have a flashlight or two with you when boating at night, especially so if you breakdown and lose power. **TowBoatUS**, **Sea Tow** and others can locate you easier if you have a light.

Once back at the marina, we will practice 3-point turns, momentum drift, and different scenarios for docking the boat. We will practice this several times until you make a few solid landings. Remember to have your fenders out and dock lines ready prior to docking. And, be sure to make the command, *"Everyone please stay seated until I have completed my docking."* The command is to everyone except perhaps a designated person who is helping with the lines. But, even for this person, command him or her to NOT jump from the boat to the dock. If you don't make a good landing, try it again. *Note: You might want a longer line available too – depending on conditions or how crowded the dock might be.* In this scenario, you bring the bow to the dock, tie the bow line to a cleat, and afterward, pull the stern around. We will go over a few different docking scenarios. Similar to flying, taking off and landing is the initial learning curve in boating. The goal is to keep a perfect incident free record. Any landing might be a good landing, but do your best to make it an impressive and safe one. Additional docking instructions are in the following pages.

DOCKING

It is wisely said, that when docking a boat, only go as fast as you are willing to allow your boat to hit the dock. In many cases the dock will be concrete, so – super slow is advised. In fact, bring your boat to a complete stop one boat length away from the dock. Take a minute to feel where the wind is coming from: it can help or hurt your docking.

I have three illustrations of docking here to show you: 1. Perpendicular docking where you are directly facing the dock, as in a fuel dock landing situation 2. Finger docking when your approach is 45 degrees to the dock, and 3. Pivot on a post (or cleat) docking.

In all three cases, I advise that you come to a complete stop one boat length or so away. In the first two examples, use forward and neutral to inch your way into position. Over time, as you gain more experience,

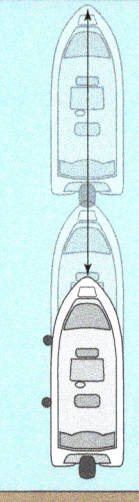

1. Stop 1-1/4 boat lengths away perpendicular to the dock.

Take note of wind direction. Have fenders out and dock lines ready.

2. Having turned the wheel all the way to the right (first), shift from neutral to forward to begin your turn.

Note: for extra precaution you can alternate between forward and neutral on your approach. But, you need to be in gear to steer, or turn.

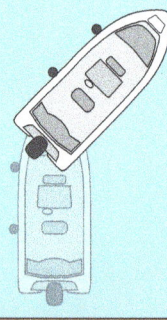

3. As your vessel comes around to the "vessel to dock" (shape) as shown, shift into neutral.

Let momentum happen until you are at the next step, a tad more parallel to the dock.

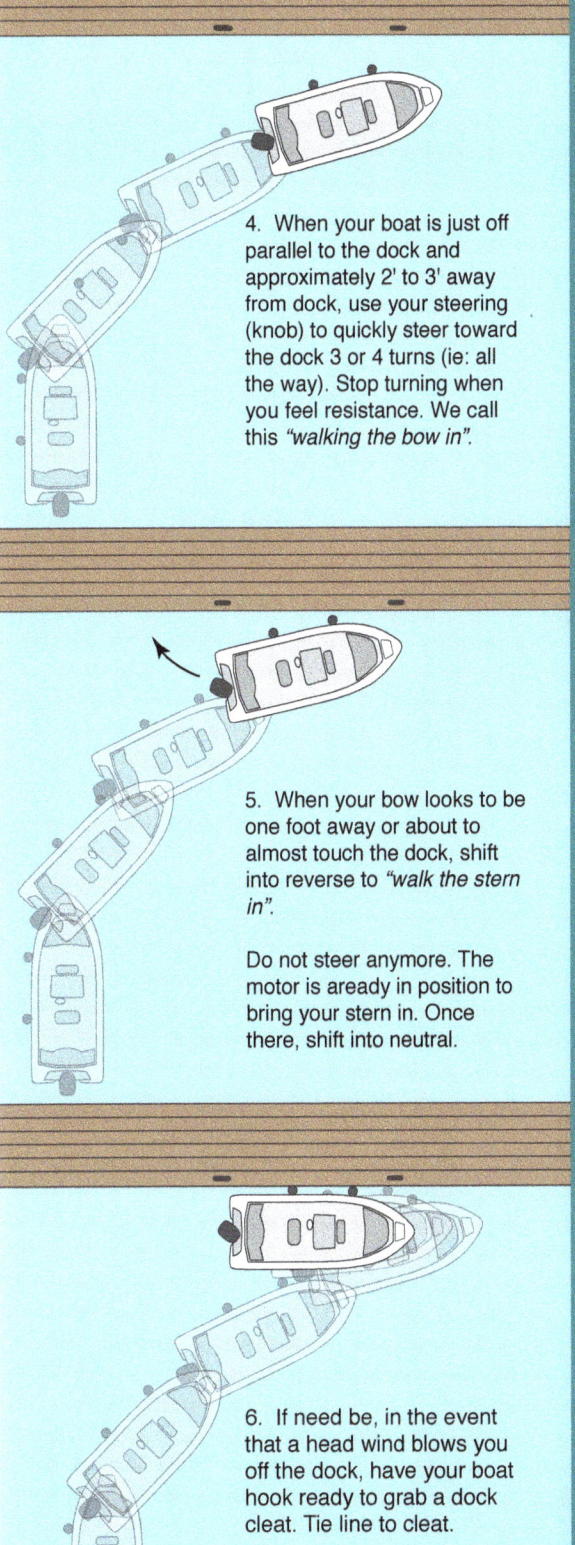

4. When your boat is just off parallel to the dock and approximately 2' to 3' away from dock, use your steering (knob) to quickly steer toward the dock 3 or 4 turns (ie: all the way). Stop turning when you feel resistance. We call this *"walking the bow in"*.

5. When your bow looks to be one foot away or about to almost touch the dock, shift into reverse to *"walk the stern in"*.

Do not steer anymore. The motor is aready in position to bring your stern in. Once there, shift into neutral.

6. If need be, in the event that a head wind blows you off the dock, have your boat hook ready to grab a dock cleat. Tie line to cleat.

you will be able to dock all in one continuous move while using the same techniques shown here in the illustration. Docking can be counter intuitive at first. There are shapes, or angles to the dock, where you perform certain tasks.

FUEL DOCK LANDING

Stop one boat length before the dock. Then turn the helm all the way to starboard in the example here. Only then, do you put your shifter into forward. When the boat is nearly parallel to the dock, and approximately 3' from the dock or wall, place the shifter into neutral. Now, steer all the way toward the dock. This will bring your bow in. When it looks as though the bow might soon touch the dock, place the shifter into reverse to bring the stern in, then into neutral. Do not touch the steering wheel during this reverse portion. The motor is already in position to bring the stern into the dock without steering. Next: fend off and tie up.

FINGER DOCK

The difference between fuel dock landing and finger dock landing is that one, fuel dock landing starts 90 degrees or perpendicular to the dock, and the other, finger dock, the approach is 45 degrees to the wall.

But, in both cases, you want to break-it-down into separate moves, rather than in one continuous move. That is to say, first get to the dock and stop. Then, position your boat 45 degrees to the finger dock.

As you approach with your bow slightly closer to the dock than your stern, and once the entire boat is in the slip area, place your boat in neutral, and use the steering knob (highly recommended) to quickly turn your motor all the way to starboard (in this example), but it is always in the direction of the dock. At this point, the use of the steering wheel is complete.

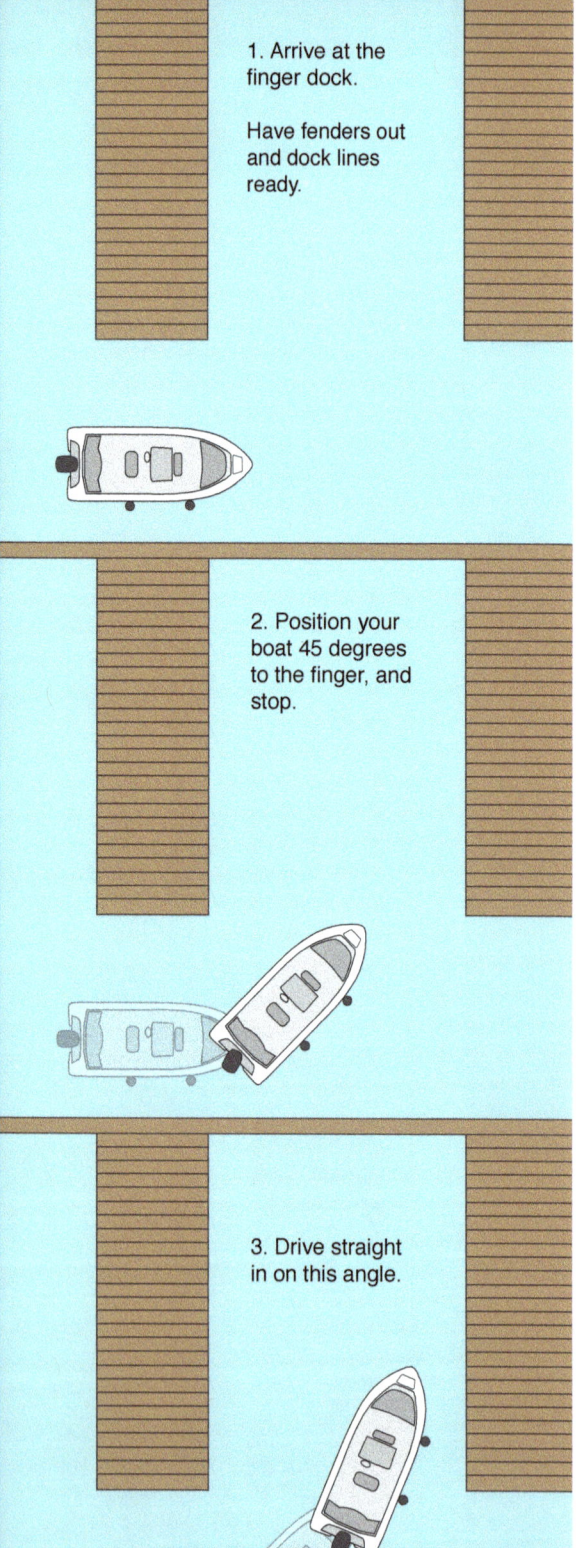

1. Arrive at the finger dock.

Have fenders out and dock lines ready.

2. Position your boat 45 degrees to the finger, and stop.

3. Drive straight in on this angle.

4. Once the dock is at the side of your boat, shift into neutral.

5. At this point steer (all the way / 4 turns) in the direction of the finger dock. This will bring your bow into the dock.

6. Shift into reverse. Do not steer. Your motor is already in position to bring your stern in. Shift into neutral. A boat hook might help. Tie up.

When it looks as though your bow is just about to touch the dock, shift into reverse for a few seconds, and then neutral. This action brings your stern into the dock, and prevents your bow from hitting.

Whatever docking method, there is no shame in using a boat hook as an assist. It is one of its designed purposes. The most important thing in docking is to take it slow. In fact, I always alternate between forward and neutral on my initial approach.

Think of docking as several different steps: Step 1. Get to the dock. Step 2. Position your boat 45 degrees to the dock. Step 3. Slowly approach the dock shifting between forward and neutral. Step 4. When your boat is inside the slip, shift to neutral. Step 5. Turn the steering wheel all the way toward the dock. Step 6. When your bow comes close to the dock, go in reverse, then neutral, then tie up.

PIVOT ON A POST

Slowly approach the dock post to lash your bow line around the post (or cleat). Have someone at the bow to fend off and wrap the bow line around the post. Leave 6' minimum of bow line between the post and your bow cleat.

Next, push off the post or cleat and steer all the way in the desired direction that you want the stern to go (starboard in this example). Remember the boat follows the direction of your motor when in reverse.

From here, shift into reverse, then shift back into neutral (each time the line tightens). You do this three or four times.

Your boat will pivot perfectly and fall into place, but it is vital to have minimum 6' of line between the post (or cleat) and your bow cleat so that the boat has freedom to make the turn.

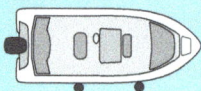

1. Have fenders out and dock lines ready.

Slowly approach post or cleat head on.

If possible have a person ready at the bow with the bow line.

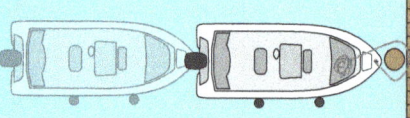

2. Shift into neutral and reverse if necessary so not to hit the post.

Lash bow line around the post.

3. Push off post about 6', and tie of bow line back to bow cleat.

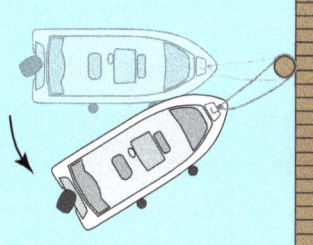

4. Steer motor towards the dock and shift into reverse.

This style of docking is very useful when A. Docking in a semi tight space between two boats, and B. When the wind is blowing your boat off the dock when unsuccessfully using other methods.

Note: only pivot on a post or cleat if they are attached to land. Do not pivot on a cleat e.g., on a floating dock, as you can drag a floating dock with you – and likely will.

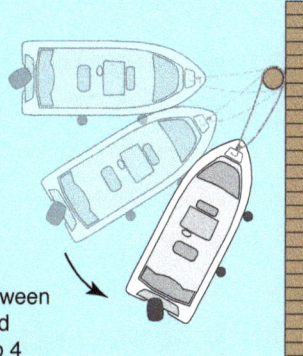

5. Shift between reverse and neutral 3 to 4 times as the boat pivots toward the dock and bow line tightens.

If you have twin outboards, you can use the pivot method coupled with shifter control. That is to say, keep your twin outboards straight. If you want the stern to move to starboard, place the starboard shifter into reverse. Place the port shifter into forward. As the line tightens, be prepared to place both shifters into neutral. This is docking twin outboards with training wheels. But, remember to stay focused, and always end your docking in neutral. Fend off and tie up.

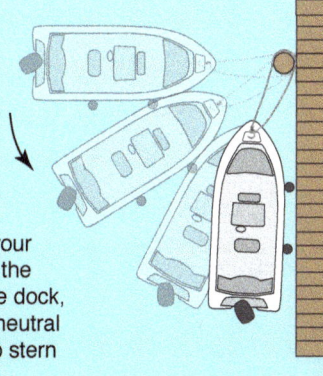

6. Once your boat is at the side of the dock, shift into neutral and tie up stern of boat.

TWIN OUTBOARDS

Two is better than one. This is true with outboard motors too. That is to say, if one motor has problems and you find yourself far offshore, you have another motor to get you back in. But, it is true too with turning around, and docking, and even steering without the use of your steering wheel.

It is fun to practice this in open water first, not near other boats or boat lifts. Think of your shifters as a futuristic steering wheel, or a video game perhaps. In any case, keep your motors straight, and do not touch your steering wheel in this exercise.

To turn to starboard (or right), place the starboard shifter into reverse and the port shifter into forward. Your boat will turn to the right. When you reverse this scenario, port in reverse and starboard in forward, your boat will turn to port. You can

Lesson: Turning around a 25' boat with twin outboards in a 40' canal.

Leave your lift in reverse and move to the center of the canal. Then, go to an open space to turn around.
Note: Motors are straight.

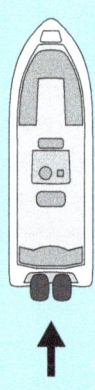

WIND

Next: turn to the right or starboard. To do this, place the starboard shifter into reverse, and the port shifter into forward.

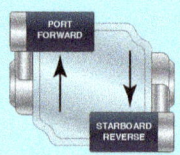

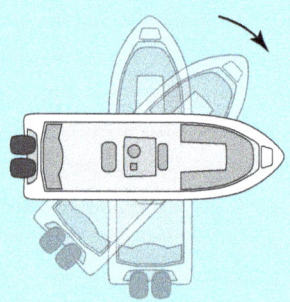

Note: You may have to increase forward or reverse speed a touch to counter the wind direction, so to stay centered in the canal.

If you have digital shifters, aka FlyByWire be extremely careful when you increase the speed as they are very sensitive.

Keep in mind: due to the wind, or other, you might need to put both shifters into neutral, and then forward or reverse to keep centered in the canal.

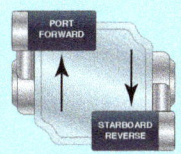

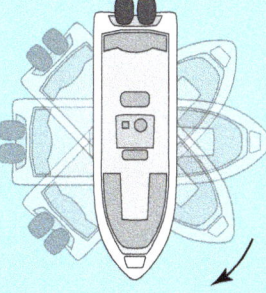

steer and maneuver a long way just using your shifters. But, you have a steering wheel, so you don't unless that is, you wish to spin around in a narrow canal. You want to achieve this by using your shifters. Your boat will spin on a dime using this technique. Let's break it down this way: Your boat is on a lift, and it is facing in–shore. You need to get it into the canal, and spun around, what do you do?

1. Turn your motors toward the middle of the canal. 2. Go reverse using one or both shifters in reverse. 3. Next, move forward into the canal where there is ample space, away from other boats and boat lifts. 4. Center your boat in the canal. 5. Take note of the wind direction and strength. 6. Place one shifter in reverse and the other in forward. Your boat will spin around.

Note: You may need to correct position to keep centered in the canal.

Continue to turn until you have achieved a 180° turn, then practice in the other direction – turn to port. Put your port shifter in reverse and your starboard shifter in forward.

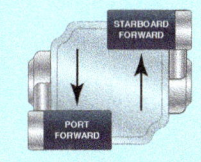

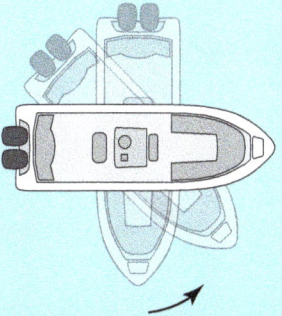

YOUR PLAYGROUND

We all have a particular playground for boating. It is based around where we live, or what boat ramp we use. Your playground is the first area that you become familiar with. Pick five places that you wish to be accomplished at getting to and from, which very well might satisfy your every boating need. It is a great focus for learning sooner than later; to familiarize yourself (and boating partner) with your surroundings – north side and south side, or the reef and the backcountry, the river and inlet, the bay to open ocean. We want you to know (not guess). And, to appreciate how the conditions vary from high tide to low tide. Just know that no two days of boating are alike. Going out and coming back on the same day can even look different, if only due to light. Remember: You are only as good as your last boating day. Keep your standards high.

PLAYGROUND DESTINATION 1

We are now ready for our first playground journey, a 4-mile trek out into the Florida Straits to **Looe Key**, an underwater marine sanctuary. That said, we do have limitations; if the wind is blowing 15 mph or more, we don't go. It is likely too choppy and the visibility is compromised as well. Single digit wind is best, but ideally no more than 12 mph. You set the waypoint to Looe Key on the GPS and prepare the vessel and passengers to get on plane. But, before you do, make sure that everything is secure.

You then say, *"I am about to get on plane, is everyone ready?"* They reply, *"ready,"* and off you go, all the while keeping a keen eye out for lobster pot buoys, debris, and marine life. Look out for birds, snorkelers and other boats too. You don't want to collide with anything. Best to remain aware at all times – not distracted and out of focus. Find a safe balance between paying attention to your surroundings, and enjoying the ride, or multitask, as you look around and always know your whereabouts, including – *where are boats.*

You read the water and notice a diagonal swell. Good thing that the swell aligns with your 45° path and track, the purple line on the GPS. Follow the purple line, your heading, all the way to Looe Key, but keep your eyes on the water too. You might see dolphin and turtle, and wish to stop. This isn't work, it's play. You just have to take part of it seriously. As you close in on Looe Key, the yellow balls or spheres indicate a SPA zone, Sanctuary Preservation Area. There are four spheres in the shape of a rectangle. Anything inside of these markers is protected; no anchoring, no fishing, harvesting, or even touching. It is an observe and enjoy area only. The GPS can only do so much. That is to say, it got you here... now what?

LOOE KEY

Looe Key, pronounced *"Lou"*, is a special place that we are very lucky to have. We are especially lucky that a family of four goliath grouper call Looe Key home. When I say goliath, I mean 8' and 500 lb+ goliath. Looe Key is for snorkelers and scuba divers alike. It is a place to marvel in the underwater world of color, and life, and beauty – however a little less so after the high water temperatures of 2023 and the bleaching that occurred. But, it is still very special.

Mooring balls with tethers, rather than anchoring, are supplied in all SPA zones for recreational use. Anchoring would damage the coral, especially with the number of boats that visit Looe Key each day and year. Boaters need to keep in mind that scuba divers are underwater too. The boater needs to keep a sharp eye out for bubbles and surfaced divers – another reason to be at idle speed within a SPA zone. Head boats from dive shops will likely call your attention to a diver. But, you should always be observant. The best approach when you arrive to the Looe Key marker is to continue out to sea beyond the mooring balls. Then, find where you might tie up, and carefully make your approach. Never cut through the reef!

Look to other boats on moorings. If their bow is facing toward the open ocean while tied up, that is the approach that you want to make to the tether. All passengers should be seated at this point, except the person with a boat hook, and the person at the helm. Approach the lanyard tied to the mooring ball slowly, shifting between forward and neutral until the line is retrieved. There is a loop at the end. The person who hooked the tether will take the bow line and

slip it through the loop at the end of the tether. Another passenger can help by taking the boat hook. The mooring tether line is left overboard and the bow line is secured back to a bow cleat. The helmsperson might shift into reverse and then neutral. Make sure that you have a good locking cleat connection. Only then, can you shut the motor off. This is when you disconnect your ignition kill switch, remember? It will remind you to raise your ladder, and bring your dive flag in before you depart. Your motor can-

not start until it is reconnected. Get in the habit of disconnecting this ignition shut-off every time that you anchor, or even every time that your ladder is down, even when drift swimming. It is a good system too, as a reminder to bring in chum after fishing, and to make certain that everything else is secure. If you decide to move from one mooring ball to another, bring your ladder up and dive flag down. Boat safe. Upon your departure, or if moving to another ball, go out to sea some before coming back in. It is not safe to ride through the mooring ball field, or to cut through from the front of the reef to the back, or vice versa. Always go around. If another boater requests to tie up to you, it is common to oblige. But, have a long dock line available so to keep the other boat a safe distance away.

A LITTLE ABOUT THE REEF

The Florida Reef Tract is the only living barrier reef in the continental United States and the third largest barrier reef in the world. It extends 350+ miles to the Dry Tortugas, with several spots along the way that reach the surface. Coral is very particular about where it grows. It requires warm, clear, salty, shallow, and sediment free conditions to survive. Pollution and fossil fuels, or green house gases play a large part in coral's demise. Coral is a living animal, meaning that it eats and it reproduces. The rock exterior that you see is the exoskeleton. The colony of life called polyps, live within

this rock exterior. Coral is in the marine science phylum, Cnidaria, (pronounced without the *"C"*), same as jellyfish and sea anemones. Coral have stinging cells called nematocysts, similar to jellyfish.

But, coral can only catch 20% of its food. So, it has a mutual relationship with an algae known as, zooxanthellae. The algae photosynthesizes, thus producing the balance of nutrients in the way of oxygen and sugar for the coral to live. Interestingly, this same algae lives within the upside-down jellyfish, known as the cassiopeia, like the constellation. It is important not to disturb or stand on coral – ever. If the zooxanthellae should be expelled from the coral for whatever reason – shockingly cold or warm water, extreme pollution, or other, coral can die. That is to say, as goes the algae, so too does the coral. There is another relationship that exists with this algae and fish, most notably, parrotfish. You should take notice of parrotfish munching on the coral. You can even hear them eat if you listen carefully. The parrotfish are eating the algae, as are numerous other fish, but not so much where they are outpacing the growth of algae. The reef is a world that strikes a balance. It is very important that we do all we can to protect it.

As previously mentioned, this particular reef is known as a groove and spur reef. There are some exceptional drone videos of Looe Key on YouTube where you will appreciate why it is called groove and spur. In this case, as with my previous hand and fingers example, your fingers represents the coral, and the groove represents sand channels between the coral. There is the front of the reef, which faces the open ocean, the crest of the reef, where you might see waves breaking over the

shallow portion, and the back of the reef, where you will see dead coral from crashing waves transitioning to a sandy bottom. The entire zone of Looe Key ranges in depth of two feet to thirty feet, and we are 4 miles out to sea. Boating offers a great opportunity to get to know your area, be it history, marine life, and ecosystem.

THE BACKCOUNTRY

A place as equally magical to the reef but altogether different is the backcountry. Imagine that our rural waterscape is your rural landscape. This is our countryside, if you will. It is a place of solitude and big sky, where one will see few other boats and hear intense quiet. But, the backcountry is more than just countryside. It is the **Great White Heron National Wildlife Refuge**. There is wildlife to be sure, and similar to countryside, it can be rugged. It can be sweet as a lamb or ferocious as a lion. That is mother nature for you. Navigating the backcountry is a whole other learning curve. The ocean can get choppy for sure, but aside from the reef there is little in the way of hazards to hit or run aground on the ocean side. Not so in the backcountry. The term "skinny water" was born in the backcountry. The slogan, *"run it, gun it, and trim it"* applies as advice – not sport. If you look down on a calm clear day, you might turnaround out of fear. It seems as though the water is one foot deep on these days, or inches, and it might be. If you are to learn boating the challenging way, it is here in the backcountry. But, what a gift it is when you learn to navigate your way to playground destinations number 2, 3, and 4 – out back. That is our next goal.

YOU'RE THE CAPTAIN

Are you watching the sun and time? Did you reapply sunscreen? Are you drinking enough water? Have you checked the radar recently? Are there any storms that you can see on the horizon? When you swim, do you put a dive flag up? Did you toss out a 50' safety line and buoy? Are you wearing fins? Who would have guessed that the list would be so long, and that you have to pay constant attention? Then, there is the outdoor activity, salt air, hot sun, and

wind that you and your passengers have to contend with. And, your passengers depend on you for smart decision making and a safe outing. Chance is the furthest thing from their minds. But, not yours. That is because, you are the captain.

NAVIGATION

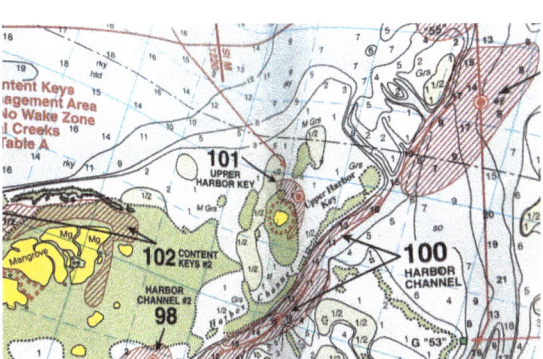

When we look at a **Top Spot** fishing chart, similar to a navigation chart but not as specific, we see the big picture. It is an aerial view same as a fly over. This is your playground, or at least some of it. You see markings for depths at low tide, markers, shoals or shallow water, hazards, and other important information; dive and fishing spots, and your route for the day. In fact, the red lines are suggested routes. An actual navigation chart allows one to measure distance, and plot a course using tools and equations. The focus of this lesson will be on GPS basics, tracks, and waypoints. It is always a good idea to take a close look at your GPS and the route that you choose to take. Look to see if there are any hazards between you and your destination, even if you do it in steps, stopping at intervals along the way. Press in Navigation > Search by Name > Looe > Navigate To > Go To, so to create a line or track to follow. See if there are any shoals, banks, or hazards along this line that might interrupt your otherwise magical day.

Recreational Boating In The Keys:
Sandbars, Snorkel, Fish, Rentals, Ramps & More

So you brought your boat to the fabulous Florida Keys - or you plan to rent one. Where do you go? How do you get there? Where are lobsters? How do you catch them? Where should you sandbar, snorkel, or fish? What are the rules? How about some waypoints? Where should you not go? Perhaps you need a hands-on boat lesson? There's no shame in that. Exactly the opposite.

Boat Rentals:
Captain Pips Marina Boat Rentals, Marathon - *305-743-4403*
Vacation Boat Rentals, Coco Plum - *305-240-9739*
Caroline's Boat Rentals, *Delivers to ramp - 305-985-0546*
Backcountry Boat Rentals, Sugarloaf - *720-738-9547*
Hands-on Boat Lesson, *(your boat / or his) - Capt Brian, 305-699-7166*

Boat Repair:
Kahuna Boat Wiring and Rigging, Marathon - *305-304-2600*
Advance Marine, BPK - *Bottom paint, fiberglass - Marty, 305-394-3985*
Ruben's Marine Service, BPK - *Ruben, 305-923-0719*
Island Time Marine, BPK, *Mobile repair Nov thru Mar - Mark - 305-432-1111*
Reel Impact Marine, Summerland Key - *Yamaha, Mercury - Joe, 305-441-7161*
Boyz N Their Toyz Marine, Cudjoe Key - *Lance, 305-745-8951*
Paradise Stitch Works LLC, *Marine Upholstery - Wendy, 608-481-3840*
Boat Shop Marine, Little Torch, *Open weekends - Yamaha, Suzuki, 772-473-6341*
D & D Custom Rods, BPK - *Rod Repair - Danielle, 954-818-9148*

Party Boats:
Marathon Mermaid, Marathon - *Sandbar, snorkel, sunset, 305-842-1492*
Sea Dog Fishing Charters, Marathon - *Head boat, 305-743-8255*
Marathon Lady, Marathon - *Party fishing boat, 305-743-5580*
Bahia Honda, Bahia Honda - *Looe Key snorkel head boat, 305-872-2353*
Captain Hooks, Big Pine Key - *Looe Key snorkel head boat, 305-872-9863*
Looe Key Dive Shop, Ramrod Key - *Looe Key snorkel head boat, 305-872-2215*
Yankee Capts, Stock Island - *Overnight fishing, 305-923-3926*
Danger Charters, Key West, *Schooner sail, eco, sunset, private, 305-304-7999*
Floridays, Key West, *Schooner sail, snorkel, sunset, events, 305-432-0046*
Conch Republic Marine Army .org, BPK, and Isla Bella - *Volunteer clean-up*

Tackle Shops:
The Tackle Box, Marathon - 305-289-0540
Jigs Bait & Tackle, Big Pine Key - 305-872-1040
Lower Keys Tackle, Big Pine Key - 305-872-7679
Cudjoe Sales, Cudjoe Key - 305-745-3667
Low Key Fisheries Cudjoe - 305-745-1311, fish market, bait
Key West Bait & Tackle, Key West - 305 -292-1961

MyRadar

Fishing:
Big Pine Shoal - 24°33.531' N, 81°20.272' W
Bahia Honda Bridge - 24°39.489' N, 81°17.352' W
Bahia Honda Reef - 24°36.864' N, 81°17.723' W
Sunset Tuna Troll - 24°33.211' N, 81°15.405' W
7 Mile Bridge - 24°41.284' N, 81°12.590' W
Backcountry (snapper) - 24°45.596' N, 81°15.897' W
Yellowtail (reef) - 24°32.999' N, 81°22.721' W

Windfinder

Fishing Times Calendar

Sandbar:
Bahia Honda (ocean) - 24°39.777' N, 81°15.340' W
Bahia Honda (bay) - 24°39.937' N, 81°16.050' W
Picnic Island - 24°38.171' N, 81°23.660' W
Tarpon Belly Key - 24°43.769' N, 81°31.251' W
Snipe Point - 24°42.062' N, 81°40.378' W
Marvin Key - 24°42.638' N, 81°38.711' W

Fish Rules

Boat US

Snorkel:
Sombrero Lighthouse - 24°37.675' N, 81°06.714' W
Looe Key Marine Sanctuary - 24°32.861' N, 81°24.156' W
Newfound Patch Reef - 24°36.931' N, 81°23.586' W

Navionics

Boat Ramps:
Marathon 33rd Street - 24°42.817' N, 81°05.739' W
Little Duck Key - 24°40.936' N, 81°13.766' W
Spanish Harbor - 24°38.968' N, 81°09.158' W
BPKRV - 24°38.889' N, 81°19.814' W
Old Wooden Bridge - 24°41.845' N, 81°20.903' W
State Road 4A - 24°40.563' N, 81°23.642' W
Blimp Road - 24°41.707' N, 81°29.977' W
Cudjoe Gardens Marina - 24°39.490' N, 81°30.341' W
Sugarloaf Marina - 24°38.840' N, 81°33.956' W
Key West City Marina - 24°33.597' N, 81°47.076' W

Nautide

Tides Near Me

US Coast Guard

PLAYGROUND DESTINATION 2

This time, we will head to the backcountry and the **Content Keys**, pronounced *"Con-tent."* To make it more interesting, we will go up one channel and return via another. The two channels are considerably different, each offering unique challenges. Rather than input a waypoint on our GPS, we will create a route, by adding turns, starting from your destination backward. We will likely cut a few corners depending on depth along the way. We will head up Pine Channel and return via Spanish Channel. Pine Channel is challenging for its shallow or "skinny water" and the route you must take to avoid damaging seagrass. There is a shortcut route, but we will navigate the outside route and approach the Content Keys from the open Gulf.

SKINNY WATER

What depth is safe for cruising through and getting on plane? It depends on the boat, but in most cases for boats in the 18' to 24' range, a depth of 3' is safe to cruise through, but maybe you are cautious and make it 3.9'. As for getting on plane, you want it to be a tad deeper, say 4'+. Remember, the bow goes up and the motor digs down as you get on plane. You need more water to protect your motor, and the sea floor. There is a big difference too, with running aground on a rising tide versus a falling tide, about five hours difference. But, this lesson is intended to teach you how NOT to run aground. Might you touch the bottom when you are going very slow through skinny water? The answer is – most definitely. But, you never want to touch bottom, or run up on a shoal to the point where you have to get pulled off. You want to familiarize yourself with your playground. Playground locations take a number of practice runs in different conditions. Record tracks on your GPS, and learn how to read the water. Familiarize yourself with conditions at high and low tide, and maybe even minus tide. And, in different light. After several trips, you should feel comfortable and confident. Polarized amber sunglasses are recommended for backcountry navigation.

Keep in mind that the chart on your GPS might say 3.9', as opposed to your depth finder, only to find out that it is closer to 1.9' when you stop. This is not an uncommon scenario in the backcountry. The charts were produced perhaps 25+ years ago. Due to hurricanes and the like, shoals move and areas become more shallow. But, this also happens during a minus tide, an extremely low tide most common around a full moon. There is also color of water that you want to become familiar with; **Brown, brown = run aground. White, white = you just might** (run aground.) **Blue, blue = sail on through. Green, green = nice and clean.** In other words, keep away from brown water. If over white sand, go slow at first to determine whether it is deep enough or very shallow. Know the difference between dark water, and water shaded from clouds. This is all rule of thumb, not rule of law. It takes practice. Your well earned experience eventually pays off.

PINE CHANNEL TO CONTENT KEYS NAVIGATION

Heading up Pine Channel, south to north, is easy if intimidating. When you pass the last homes on Little Torch Key, there is a shoal in front of the homes on the north side. Pass them several hundred yards to the north, before turning to port, or west into 2' water. This is a good time to trim your motor up some and remind yourself to "believe" – and to keep on plane. Don't stop. There is a straight away from here. Keep 150 to 200 yards off the Torch Keys as you head north. The first island to your starboard has a few PVC markers off to its southwest, marking a rather long shoal. There is one PVC marker with a traffic cone atop it that you want to keep just to starboard as you pass it. From there, it is a two mile straight away in mostly 3' deep water. Most any small to medium size boat, 12' to 24' can take this route. It only looks intimidating. At the top of the straight away, there is another PVC pipe, that might not be visible at high tide. In any case, once you are parallel to this starboard side island, begin your turn and aim for 2 o'clock, keeping 100 yards or more north of the island. When you get to the middle of the island, it is time to turn again, to port, and head due north. You may or may not see two more PVC pipes that you keep just to starboard. After the second pipe or 200 yards, turn right to 2 o'clock, toward the channel. You are now in the backcountry of the FL Keys.

After a brief stop, follow the deeper water. You can go northwest and around some shoals, or north in-between the shoals that are clearly marked on your GPS. I take the north route.

You are heading toward Upper Harbor Key. It is necessary to follow your GPS and zig-zag around a shoal or two before making it to the channel. Follow the deep water northeast, and then north leaving Upper Harbor Key to your port side. A few hundred yards ahead on the port side is a 15' spot and a channel that cuts through a shoal. *Note: There is a sandbar to port, where you can beach your boat at low tide, but know whether it is a rising or falling tide.* From here, go west for 200 yards, and as your GPS will tell you, dogleg around to the right, heading north for another 100 yards before turning left, or west, into 7' water. The bottom is sandy and often presents itself as such sticking out from the very shallow and dark turtle grass bottom to either side. Follow the white. You are now in the open Gulf.

Cut back southwest between Upper Harbor Key and the Content Keys, all the while minding your depth. Head toward 4' - 10' water depth and work your way in until you have East Content Key and West Content Key at an equal distance, favoring West Content Key some. There is a 3.9' spot which is the opening to "the passage." Low tide navigation is of course more challenging than high tide navigation, but it is perhaps more beautiful too, exposing shoals, and presenting more opportunity for bird viewing. Even though this is the outside route, it is one that you might wish to experience a few times with someone who knows it – prior to going it alone.

Just inside the passage to the immediate west is a lovely lagoon, and inside the lagoon – a mangrove corridor to paddle. You want it to be a rising tide here as the depths at high tide are only two feet deep, suitable only for flats boats, bay boats, and some skinny water center consoles up to 23'. The approach to the lagoon is best achieved on plane, (and trimmed up) with a zig-zag or two tossed in. Deeper into the passage, at low tide, a nice beach is exposed. This beach is on the south side of West Content Key – best navigated to on a diagonal track once parallel to the lagoon. It is possible that your boat bottom will touch on the way, so avoid dark spots and stay over sand. It is always a good idea to drop two anchors when beaching a boat. One to keep you on the beach, and the other to pull you off when it comes time to go. Boats larger than 24' should probably go no further than the passage itself. You can enjoy the east side shallows for a dip.

ABOUT THE CONTENT KEYS

The Content Keys are a favorite destination for many. Birdlife abounds, and marine life too. You will see guides poling through the flats targeting tarpon, bonefish, and permit. But, be sure to keep a good distance away. The fish they are spying are very skittish. And, the client onboard is likely enjoying a bucket list moment. The Content Keys are great for loners and socializers alike. Another beach, on the Gulf side of west Content Key, is rugged and rarely visited. One can snorkel here and explore the beach, but you will need wet shoes due to its rocky bottom. It is especially beautiful here during a minus tide. There are sea cucumbers, rays, nurse sharks, and tarpon. One can beach, explore, snorkel, lobster, fish, paddle through mangroves, and picnic. In short, it is a great place to spend the day, and even the night, when the conditions are right.

CONTENT KEYS TO SPANISH CHANNEL NAVIGATION

The return is the same but completely different. That is how it can look as the light of day changes – completely different. But, perhaps more beautiful too. We will go back through the same Upper Harbor Key cut and dogleg, but only to the sandbar. To return via Big Spanish Channel, continue straight, leaving the sandbar to your starboard. You are heading east. The open Gulf is to your port. The water is 5' deep here. You are looking for a green marker in the distance, likely silhouetted by the island behind it. This is channel marker "53". *Note: It is not very common for people to go up one channel and back another because you end up a good distance from where you started.*

Pine Channel is Little Torch Key and Newfound Harbor territory, while Big Spanish Channel takes you in the direction of No Name Key and Bahia Honda Key. The two channels are ten miles apart. Only guides generally travel various channels, but it is a good opportunity to learn a couple of different routes, and to take in some beautiful scenery.

We are here because of the markers. Not because they are very challenging, but you rarely see this many markers in one spot. And, rather than the red / right / return rule – since we are heading in from the Gulf, not the ocean, we leave all red markers to port and the green markers to starboard. This is a very good exercise to compare what you see with the naked eye, to what your GPS tells you. Your GPS is telling you that a given marker is where it is because there is a shoal on the other side of this man made channel and marker – that you don't want to hit. You want to think ahead, and keep in mind, red / left / return, or green / right / return – until you make it all the way through. I've seen boats not make it.

After that, it is clear sailing, or motoring. Some sailboats do make their way through this route because it is the southernmost, Seven Mile Bridge ocean side to Gulf crossing via the Intracoastal Waterway (ICW), until you get to Key West, In general, larger sailboats will wait for a rising tide to make this leg of the journey.

Once through the markers we can take the channel all the way to Bahia Honda Key. We can also cut over to Bogie Channel and Big Pine Key. There are very few obstacles along the way, but not none. Both routes are easy to navigate after you've done it a few times. And, that is the point of this exercise – practice and familiarity. Those of you who live in the Lower Keys, and snowbirds, now have two very different and very beautiful playground destinations to start your list. For those of you not from the area, do the same where you boat. Practice your routes, and before long it becomes second nature. You don't have to go far or fast to enjoy boating. The moment that you get on the water, you are already a world away. Take the time to stop and enjoy it, even if only on a kayak. There are some pretty hardy people who paddle great distances by kayak, and camp out too. Add a kicker motor and a pontoon to your kayak and – unlimited possibilities.

Though I have listed but two Florida Keys playground destinations here, the lesson is easily transferable to where you live. On a recent visit to Long Island, NY, I was reminded of the many playground destinations there too – Larchmont, NY to Port Jefferson, Sag Harbor, NY to Montauk. Or, Douglaston, NY to Louie's restaurant in Port Washington, a longtime favorite of mine. Another special memory was when I learned to navigate down the East River to the Statue Of Liberty. What a thrill! Your destination might be just across the bay to enjoy nature sounds, lunch, or a simple day of fishing. Like anything, the more you do it, the better you get at it. You might eventually work your way to boating at night, or a multi-day expedition, like Douglaston to Montauk, or perhaps, The Great Loop, up the Hudson River, through the Erie Canal, and down the Mississippi. An experienced (and patient) boater can follow the template of this lesson, and show you how to get started.

BUOYS AND MARKERS

Buoys and markers are traffic signals. They offer directions and information and otherwise identify dangerous or controlled areas. As a recreational boater you should familiarize yourself with markers.

Red colors, red lights, and even numbers (2, 20, 52) represent the right side of the channel as a boater enters from the open sea or heads upstream. When in doubt, check shoal locations on your GPS. Trust your GPS!

Green colors, green light, square shape, and odd numbers generally indicate the left side of the channel as a boater enters from the open sea or heads upstream.

Red and green colors, and or lights, indicate the preferred (primary) channel. If green is on top, the preferred channel is to the right as a boater enters from the open sea, or heads upstream. If red is on top, the preferred channel is to the left. Nuns are coned shaped buoys with even numbers. Cans are cylindrical shaped buoys with odd numbers. Lighted buoys use the lateral marker colors and numbers discussed above. *Note: These buoys have matching colored lights.* Day markers are permanently placed signs attached to structures, such as posts. Common day markers are red triangles with even numbers or green squares with odd numbers. Refer to **Boating Skills and Seamanship** for thorough information.

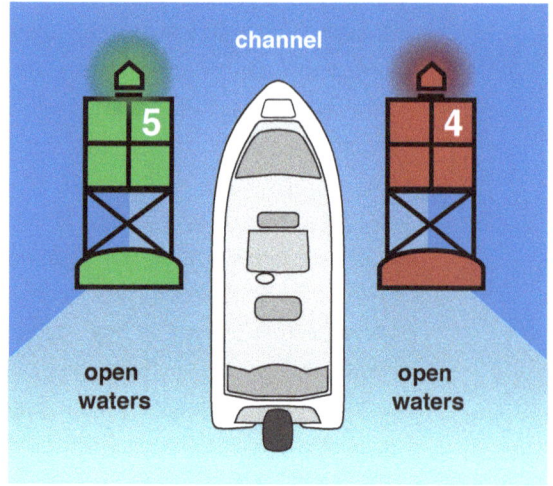

The **Intracoastal Waterway** (ICW) is a chain of channels that provide an inland passage along the US east coast. Buoys and markers in this system are identified by yellow symbols and serve a dual purpose: navigation aids for both the lateral system of markers and the ICW. Yellow triangles should be kept on the starboard of your vessel. Yellow squares should be kept on the port side of your vessel.

Non lateral markers (often times cylindrical white buoys) include information; square indicates where to find food, supplies, Controlled; circles may indicate speed limit, no anchoring, and the like.

Exclusion: crossed diamonds indicate off limits to all vessels such as swimming areas, dams. Danger; diamonds warn of dangers such as rocks, shoals, wildlife, and construction. Always proceed with caution. Mooring buoys are always white with a blue band, where vessels are allowed to anchor. Safe water markers are white with red vertical stripes and mark mid channels or fairways. They may be passed on either side. White buoys with black vertical stripes indicate an obstruction to navigation. Do not pass between these buoys and the nearest shore. Lobster

and crab pot buoys are not navigational aids but you at least know that a boat can get to them. It means that there is navigable water here. Take note of where there are no lobster or crab pot buoys. It is a good bet that it is a very shallow area, and should be avoided.

VHF Radio: you should always monitor weather developments, as the odd storm can appear out of nowhere. Additional VHF channels are used to communicate with other boaters, and to summon help. They include channels: 6, 9,13,16, 22, 24-28, 68, 69, 71 and 78.

REGISTERING YOUR VESSEL

You must have a FL certificate of registration and valid decal unless you are a non motorized vessel less than 16', or non motorized canoe, kayak, rowing skull of any length (for inland and open waters). Registration identification numbers must be affixed to both sides of the bow, where it can be seen clearly. Numbers must read from right to left, be contrasting block letters and numbers at least 3" in height. Letters must be separated from the numbers by one space. Decal must be affixed to the port side within 6" of the registration number. The decal may precede or follow the number. It is illegal to operate your vessel otherwise. In addition, while operating your boat, you must carry the original registration with you. The hull ID number is a 12 digit number assigned by the manufacturer to vessels built after 1972. You should write down your HIN number and keep it in a secure place separate from your vessel in the event that your vessel (or trailer) is stolen. A certificate of title proves ownership. A certificate of registration is valid for one or two years, expiring on the last day of the month prior to the owners birth. The owner of a FL registered vessel must notify the tax collectors office within 30 days if he or she changes address, if the vessel is sold, stolen, destroyed, abandoned, or lost. Check laws where you live.

REQUIRED NAVIGATION LIGHTS

Power driven, including sailing vessels under power: if less than 65.6 feet long, the required lights are red and green sidelights viewable from a distance of at least two miles away, or if less than 39.4 feet, viewable by at lease one mile away. In addition, an all around white light, or both a masthead light and a stern light. These lights must be viewable from a distance of at least two miles away on a dark clear night. The all around white light, or the masthead light, must be at least 3.3 feet higher than the side lights.

UNPOWERED VESSELS / SAILBOATS UNDER SAIL

If less than 65.6 feet, the vessel must exhibit red and green sidelights visible for a distance of at least two miles away, or if less than 39.4 feet, visible from at least one mile away, and a stern light visible from at least two miles away. If less than 23 feet long, these vessels should, if practical, exhibit the same lights required for unpowered vessels less than 65.6 feet in length. If not practical, have on hand at least one lantern or flashlight shining a white light 45° to the bow / air so to avoid any chance of collision.

TYPE B: Liquids / Grease: gasoline, oil, gre ase, tar, oil-based paint, lacquer, flammable gases

FIRE EXTINGUISHERS

All non exempt vessels are required to carry a Type B (for gas) USCG approved fire extinguisher on board. Approved types of fire extinguishers must display Marine Type USCG approved, followed by the size and type. Only USCG fire extinguishers are legal for use on vessels, and should be placed in an accessible area away from the engine.

VISUAL DISTRESS SIGNALS (VDS)

Vessels less than 16' must carry at least three night signals if operating between sunset and sunrise: flares, flashlight, horn. An orange flag is an additional day distress signal. Vessels 16' and greater must carry at least three day signals and three night signals. It is prohibited to display distress signals on the water, except when assistance is required.

LITTLE USED BUT POTENTIALLY HELPFUL

All vessels are required to carry sound producing devices such as a whistle or a horn that is audible for at least a half mile. Larger vessels also may be required to carry a bell or gong.

One short blast tells other boaters
"I intend to pass you on my port side"

Two short blasts tells other boaters
"I intend to pass you on my starboard side"

Three short blasts tells other boaters
"I am backing up"

In restricted visibility, the signal is:
One prolonged at intervals of no more than two minutes

For sailing vessels in restricted visibility:
One prolonged blast and two short blasts

Warning: coming around a blind bend:
One prolonged blast

Distress:
Five (or more) short rapid blasts

DIVER DOWN FLAG

A diver down flag is required by FL law whenever scuba divers and snorkelers are in the water. It is prudent when swimming too. Boaters must make a reasonable effort to keep 300' away in open water and 100' in rivers and restricted channels, and must proceed no faster than to maintain headway (idle speed). Conversely, divers and snorkelers must make every effort to stay within 300' of their flag in open water, and 100' in restricted waters. *Note: The diver down flag must be removed when a diver, snorkeler or swimmer is not in the water.* Flags must be at least 20"x24" and stiffened with wire to keep its shape. It must be clearly displayed. If on a tow buoy along with the snorkeler, the flag must be at least 12"x12".

UNLAWFUL OPERATION

Reckless or careless operation, including improper storage of water skis, anything that can endanger life or limb, boating in restricted areas without regard to other boaters – speed, wakes, dive flag, and exceeding the maximum weight limit of the vessel.

BOATING ACCIDENTS

Do not drink and operate a boat. Same as with an automobile, intoxication limit is .08. It is said that one beer on the water, is equivalent to three beers on land. This is due to sun and wind exposure, and salt air dehydration. Regardless, drinking and driving is illegal. In the event of a boating accident, the boat operator must stop his or her vessel immediately at the scene unless this action endangers his or her vessel, crew, or passengers. If you are in, or see a boating accident, give assistance (good samaritan). If need be, give his or her name, address, and vessel ID number to the operator and or owner of the damaged property.

Vessel operators involved in an accident must report the accident by the quickest means possible if the accident has resulted in death, disappearance, or any injury causing medical attention beyond first aid, or damage to a vessel and other property of $2000 or more. The report of the accident must be made to FWC 888-404-3922, or the sheriff of the county where the accident occurred. Failure to report an accident, and failure to render first aid are criminal offenses.

You obviously cannot discard trash, oil, or any other hazardous substances. You should always do your part to pick up any floating bags, bottles, and styrofoam whenever possible. If your vessel is 26' or greater, you must display a 5"x8" placard stating the Federal Water Pollution Control Act's law. If your vessel discharges oil or hazardous substances into the water call 800-424-8802. In addition, vessels 26' and greater, must display a 4"x9" placard to notify passengers and crew about garbage discharge restrictions. It is illegal to dump garbage, refuse, or plastic in FL waters.

Know where to go: running aground on FL seagrass, or where you live, can result in a hefty fine and damage to your boat. If in the Keys, if you see a prop scar, and you might add to it: 1. Stop and raise your motor, 2. Pole into deeper water, or 3. Walk your vessel out of the shallow area or seagrass bed.

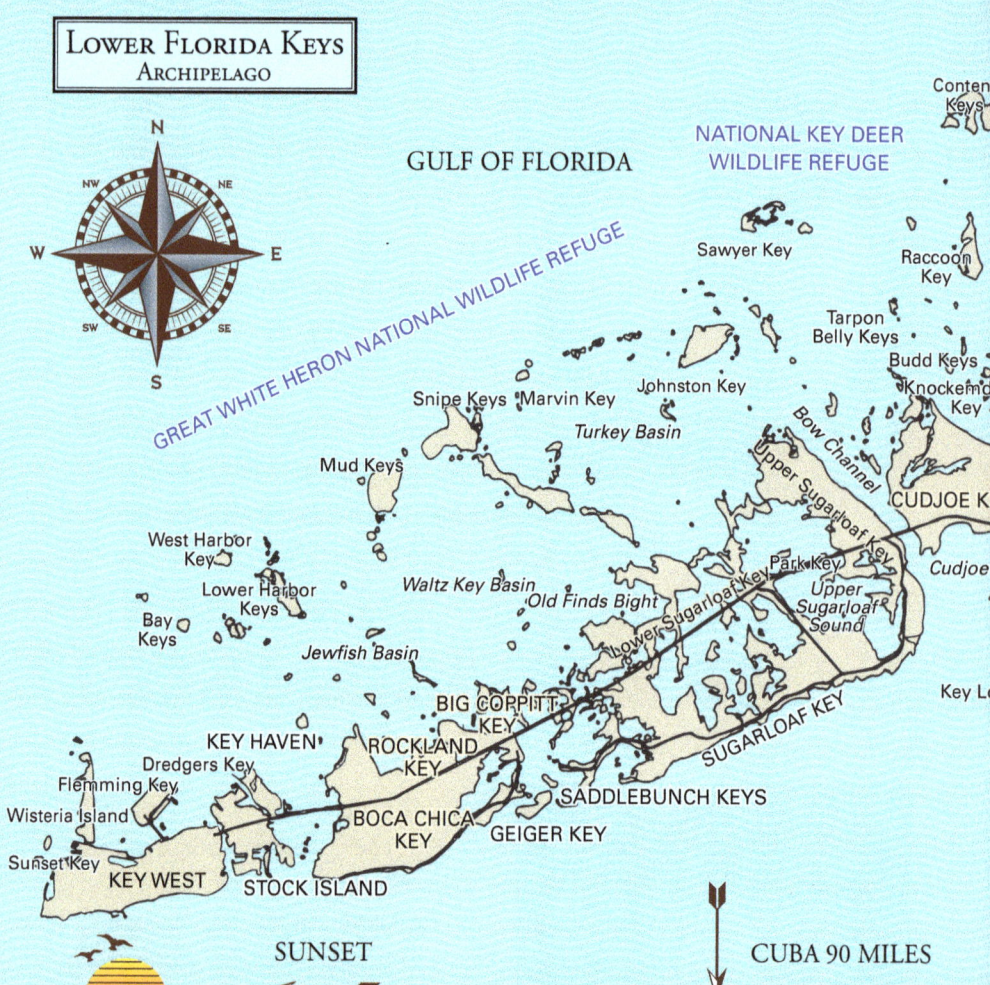

Do you know your Keys from Marathon to Key West?

Quiz each other, and see. Marathon, Little Duck, Missouri, Ohio, Bahia Honda, Scout Key, Big Pine Key. And, don't forget Park Key, if only a causeway – which connects Upper and Lower Sugarloaf Key. That said, the causeway between Big Pine Key and Little Torch Key has no name.

Marathon to Key West: Due West or Due South?

Key West is the southernmost point in the Continental US, and some 60 miles closer to Cuba than Miami. But, when the sun is setting, and you are headed toward Key West, the sun is in your eyes because you are headed west, not south. It is the same when you are headed toward Marathon from the Lower Keys at sunrise. The sun is in your eyes, because you are headed east, not north. Some can argue that it is east northeast and west southwest, but not north/south. Even though our buses say Northbound and Southbound, and the radio stations report traffic as such, US 1 in the Keys is mostly east / west.

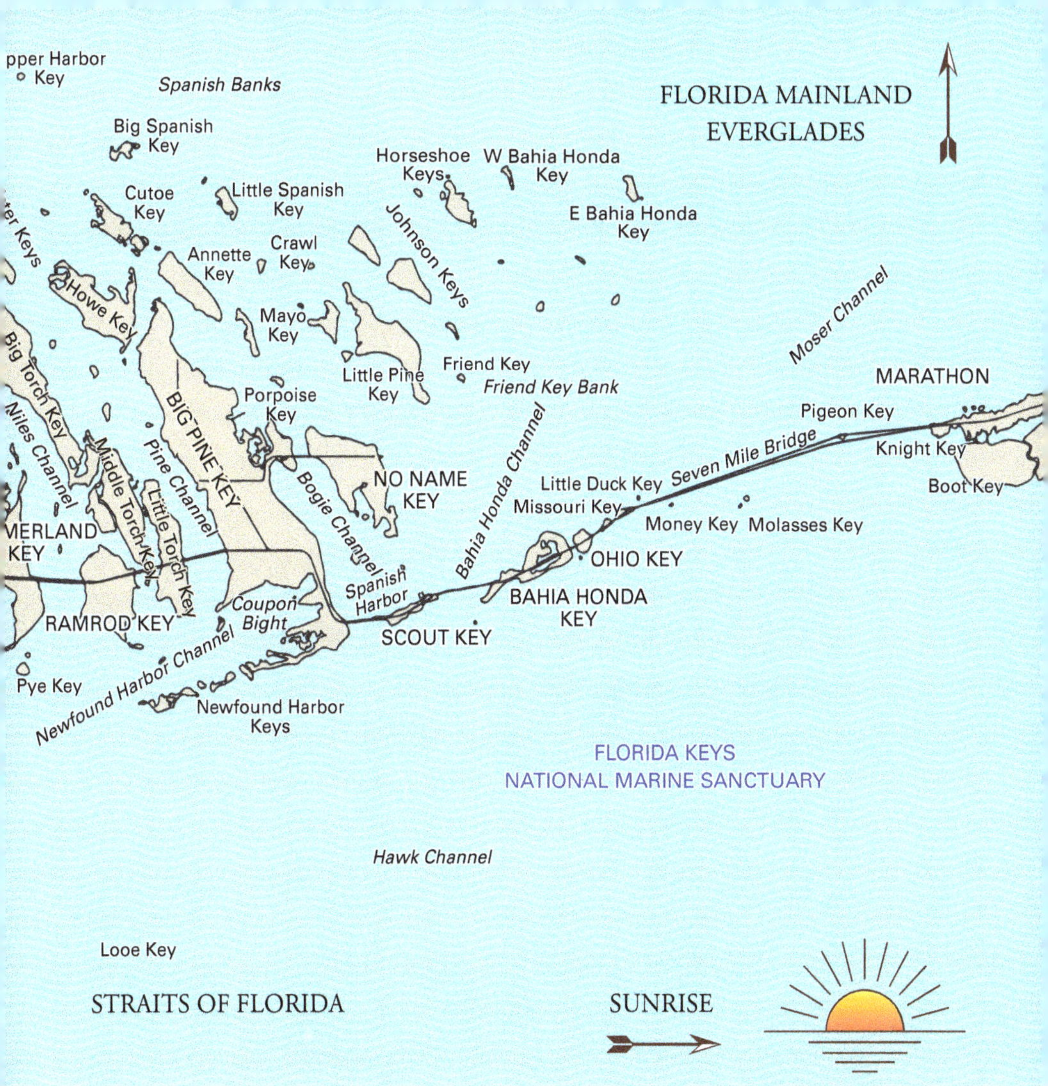

Ocean Side vs. Gulf Side / Bay Side

The ocean side, aka the Straits Of Florida (not the Atlantic), is the body of water in between the Atlantic Ocean and the Gulf Of Mexico, and in between the Florida Keys and Cuba – which is 90 miles due south of Key West. The Gulf side, north of the Keys and just beyond the islands of the backcountry is the Gulf of Mexico.

The Tale Of Two Tides

One particular phenomenon regarding the Straits Of Florida and The Gulf Of Mexico is that not only does the Florida Keys archipelago act as a divider of these two bodies of water, but that the tides are opposite one another. The Gulf tide rises north to south, and the Straits Of Florida tide rises south to north, or toward one another. The tides recede away from one another rather than flow in one continuous direction. In fact, it can be high tide in Bogie Channel at both the US 1 bridge and the No Name Key bridge one day, and the next week, high tide at one bridge and low tide at the other, or vice versa. This is due to the opposing tides.

YOU: STEER IT, ANCHOR IT & DOCK IT   71

MAINTENANCE

Boating maintenance used to routinely happen in 100 and 300 hour increments. Yamaha has combined most all maintenance to 100 hours, and otherwise annually (internal anodes, thermostats). But, 300 hours is the average amount of time put on a recreational boat in a season. If you think about it, four 4-hour days per week is 64 hours per month. If you multiply that by five months, it comes to 320 hours. In warmer climates maintenance can be a two, or four time event. At 100 hours, it is time to change your oil, oil filter, and lower unit lube. You should also change your fuel water separator, spark plugs, and impeller. Check your steering trim and tilt fluids too, grease your prop shaft, and top off grease nipples. This is an annual maintenance for many, but for frequent boaters, the 100

hour maintenance can come quickly, and does. It is very important to keep track of your running hours in order to stay on top of your 100 hour maintenance. That said, nowadays with FlyByWire or digital controls, hours are kept for you. But, maintenance is not just a 100 hour event. It is a daily observation to look, listen, keep a list, and repair as needed. Most all what you need to know, can be found on YouTube. It will bring out the mechanic in you, you never knew, and save you a bundle too. It is wise to inspect under your cowling or motor cover from time to time for dry-rotted hoses, salt build-up, hose clamp tightness, rusted parts, and so forth. WD-40 and CRC are good lubricants to spray over your motor.

Additional maintenance needs generally include attention to switches, wire contacts, wire brushing battery terminals, and changing internal anodes – all to keep your boat happy and running. *Note: battery life is generally 3 to 4 years. That is when you should change it / them.* I keep a "boat maintenance" page in my Notes on my iPhone. It is essential to have a tool kit or two, one for electrical: fuses, wire connectors, wire cutter, crimper, heat shrink, mini torch, and wire. Another kit should include basic tools: standard and metric sockets, pliers, adjustable wrench, screwdriver, wire, and zip ties.

You should also know how to troubleshoot common problems like, boat won't start: it has to be spark, fuel, or compression. Or, per-

haps it's a loose battery cable, or disconnected kill switch. No GPS or trim tabs? Likely a loose wire or a bad switch. No water is coming out of your motor: use a wire to clean the tracer out. It could be a bad impeller, or loose water pump gasket. A bad bilge pump is not good. If you keep your boat in the water, the bilge pump HAS to be working. Often times, the brushes go bad and you can replace the motor only, but probably better to replace the whole pump as it is only a $5 difference, and you have to re-wire anyway. If done while your boat is in the water, be sure to close the seacock, or your boat can sink. Regular maintenance is key to boating. Remember, nothing survives saltwater conditions, not stereo speakers, USB connectors, or any connector for that matter. Better to flush mount GPS units rather than unplug on a daily basis – too much wear and tear. Most important perhaps is regular 100 hour oil, lube, and filter change. Self maintaining is a not especially fun, but it can prove very rewarding, and it definitely saves you time and money.

YOUTUBE AS MENTOR

It is helpful too, to familiarize yourself with various other lessons on *YouTube: how to anchor, how to dock, how to trailer, how to troubleshoot, and so forth.* YouTube has always come through for me with all sorts of information. It has saved me money time and again, hundreds of dollars per boat per year by teaching me to do basic maintenance myself. In any situation, if you don't know it, YouTube it first. Granted, it can be a little intimidating: taking the lower unit off of the motor to replace the impeller, but it is no more difficult than learning to bake a cheesecake – truly. Take advantage of the technology that is available to us. To learn more about, adjusting your idle, changing your oil, or fixing your trailer, taking apart your carburetor = YouTube. *PS: YouTube is not a sponsor of mine – yet. I do often think about making a* **YouTube U** *T-shirt.*

It is not true what they say, *"the best two days of owning a boat are the day that you buy it, and the day that you sell it."* I have never found that to be the case. Every day on the water is a good day. And, like this lesson suggests, with proper prior preparation, bad experiences happen less often. As for hourly mechanic rates, the average is $150+ per hour, plus parts. You want a person who will get the job done right – that is all. And, hopefully within the same week. You do not want a deal or a favor, where you feel that you owe them. You just want it done right. Because the alternative is a big headache. It is said, that *"a boat is a hole in the water that you throw money into."* If you regularly maintain your boat, you can greatly minimize the size of the hole.

ANCHORS

Your selection of a particular type of anchor is very dependent on where you boat and the conditions that exist: rocky, muddy, or sandy bottom, light current or strong current, waves versus flat, and wind or no. There are several different types of anchors to choose from. The most common anchors in the Keys are **Danforth** (fluke), **Grapnel** (grappling), and **Bruce** (plow or claw). The ideal is to carry two different types of anchors for different situations, e.g., muddy and rocky, even though this is not the common practice on small recreational boats. You should choose your anchor depending on your common outing. And, important to know, is a special rig that prevents losing a grapnel, Bruce, or plow anchor.

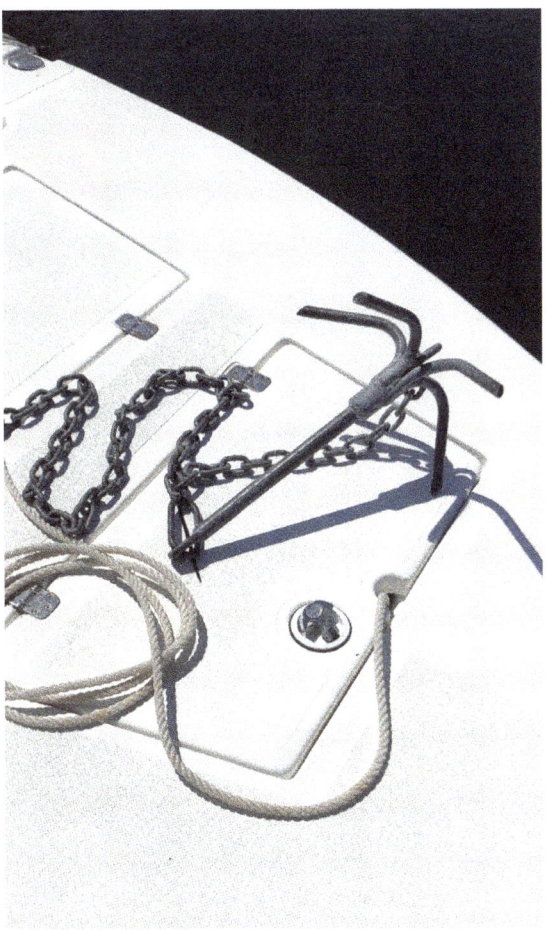

The rig I speak of attaches the chain to the bottom of the anchor, as opposed to the top. And, then zip ties to the top shackle, as if attached to the top, but instead acts as a break-away. By doing so, it enables a hopelessly stuck anchor to flip around and come out in the opposite direction. You will never lose an anchor with this set-up. That said, you do want to secure the bitter end of your anchor line to somewhere in the boat. This is a good time to review the extremely handy, bowline knot. *See page 82.* In short, a Danforth anchor is the most widely used anchor for sandy and mud bottom conditions. A Grapnel or grappling anchor is good in rocky areas. That said, I now mainly use a plow anchor for two reasons: 1) it holds in both rock and grass, and 2) it doesn't do as much damage to the seafloor. If the anchor gets stuck in rocks, which happens often – when pulled hard enough, the zip tie will break and cause the chain to flip around, pulling the anchor from the bottom in the opposite direction, thus freeing the anchor. Many novice boaters lose at least one anchor in their boating life, but you don't have to. Whenever possible, find a sand patch and lower the anchor and chain rather than throw it in. Lowering the anchor helps to prevent

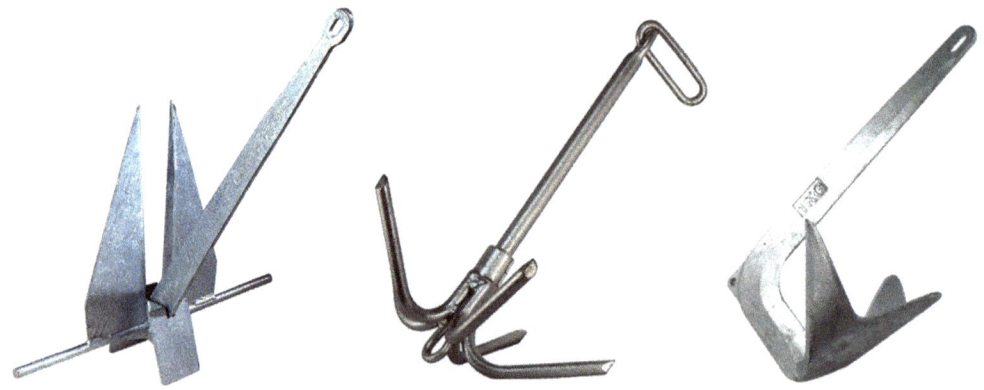

Left to right: Danforth, Grapnel, and Bruce anchors

your chain from fouling around the claw. It also allows the anchor to lay down as it was designed to do (which is why a chain is attached in the first place). The chain adds weight to the anchor and lays it down. You then feed out the line, also known as rode, and count individual lengths 3' to 5' at a time until you are at a 5:1 or 7:1 scope ratio. If you are in five feet of water, you want to feed out 25' of scope. If it is windy or there is strong current, try 7:1 scope or 35'. If 7:1 doesn't work, you might have to go to 10:1. In most all situations, when your anchor is dragging, feed out more line, then take a wrap around the cleat and wait for it to set. If it still doesn't grab, you will have to pull up your anchor and try again. You know that the anchor is set when the bow is pointing straight toward the anchor – and not sideways to it. You can feel the set or drag when you grab the line.

In all situations, keep the motor running, especially near a bridge and in current until your anchor is set. Feed the line out to the proper scope (length of rope depending on depth of water and current), and then take a 360° wrap around the bow cleat.

Make absolutely sure to keep your feet and legs away from the anchor line as you feed it out, and that your hands don't get caught in the cleat as you take a wrap. This wrap is also a brake. It is at this point where the weight of the boat against the current, is 100% on the cleat, and not on your hands. Tie off your cleat: figure eight over the back of the cleat, then the front, and lock it. If there is a lobster pot buoy, mooring or other drag indicator nearby, make a mental note of your approximate distance to it. Glance over to it from time to time, to see whether you are drifting or dragging. All things boating takes awareness. You need to be aware of your surroundings, other boats, and markers. It is all for your benefit and safety. Retrieving your anchor can be a challenge, and at times, dangerous. Automatic winches called a windless can pull your anchor up with a push of a button. But, most small recreational boats don't have this convenience. In all other cases, an anchor is retrieved the old fashion way, you pull it up with your back, legs, and arms. On occasion, the anchor gets stuck, which is expected.

So, you have to pull a little harder. But, be careful not to slip when it suddenly releases. It is best to stay low. You might pull so hard that the zip tie breaks – not uncommon. As previously mentioned, it is helpful to have one person drive forward toward the anchor, while the other person gathers the rode back into the anchor locker.

If your anchor is hopelessly stuck, you will need to use the power of the boat to break it free. In this case, the boat should drive 30 degrees off the direction of the anchor very slowly until it breaks free. This is similar to the retrieving ball (but without it). Afterward, place the boat back in neutral, and once you are away from hazards like a bridge, retrieve it. Have a zip tie at the ready so that you can re-rig the anchor right away. You always want the anchor ready. Don't forget: the anchor is a emergency device

too. It is one of the first things you select when you have motor problems: Look around for other boats, get your boat out of the channel, and drop your anchor. At this point you are safe and secure. You can now try to assess why your motor stopped or stalled, and if need be, radio for help. Dropping an anchor can also prevent you from running aground.

YOU MAKE THE CALL

If you set off on a beautiful day, only to discover that the conditions are not as ideal as you had hoped, a new approach must be found. There will be a time when it is too late, and you are in a "Dear God" situation. Deal with it the best you can. You have to read the water and become one with it. Your speed is a key factor as it controls your timing; rising up over the wave, and then riding down the wave, ideally at the same speed the wave is falling. If it still doesn't feel safe, you should approach the wave at a 45° angle, all the while, reading the waves, and zig-zag to and from – until you are safe. I have been there on a few such occasions.

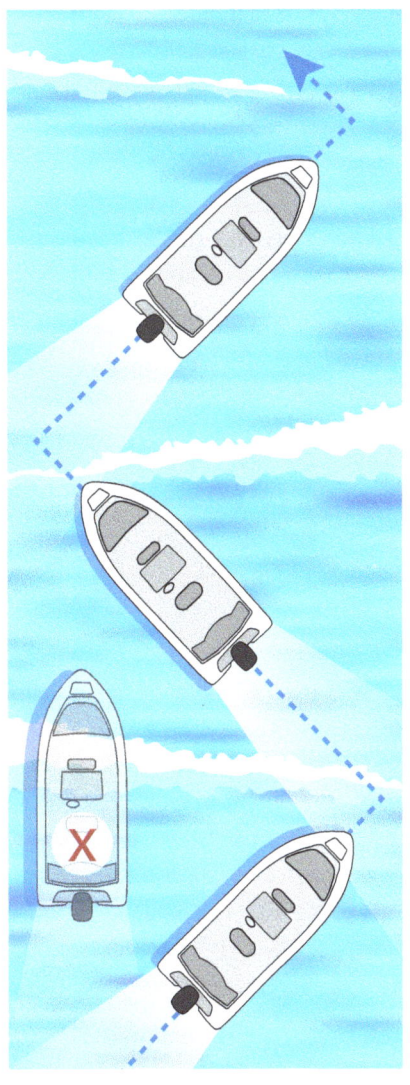

There are boating days and non-boating days. Live to see another boating day. Common sense and judgment call is the same thing. You will experience many days where you have to make a tough, but right call. If caught in the mix of it, already far out, never let waves hit you on the side or beam. It could result in a capsize. You also don't want to take water over the bow. In a worst case scenario, most often in heavy weather, people have been known to toss an anchor off the stern, not to hit bottom, but to add weight and drag. They might fill their livewell too. It helps to keep steerage. You should always be wearing a PFD (life jacket) in extreme conditions, and consider a lifeline tether too. A particularly discomforting scenario is when you lose visibility due to fog or heavy rain. You need to be ready for these instances too. You should already know the depths around you, where your lee shore is, where rocks and shoals are in the area, listen for other boats, and have a horn handy. In this case, it is a good thing that you learned the sound signals.

WEATHER

Fortunately, fog and rain eventually pass, but that doesn't comfort you in the moment. If you see a sign of fog, a big storm brewing and lightening, it is best to get somewhere safe. But, there is often little time. Maintain a look out far from engine noise, so to listen for other vessels. Do what you can to get clear of the channel and shipping lane. Monitor your radio. Take note of your latitude and longitude coordinates, and if necessary, radio for assistance. You should always remain observant; know where you are at all times. Not unlike a man overboard drill, it is important to be prepared for such a moment.

These are scary situations that you can laugh about later, but it is no laughing matter in the moment. Sometimes, in fact, it is nothing short of frightening. I am reminded of a time... when blue skies turned dark, then thunder. And, I was on a charter with 4 children and two moms. All the while, the MyRadar app read clear. Then, two waterspouts and lightening bolts appeared in the near distance, the direction we were going. It was also a minus tide, and little leeway. So, we waited it out – and got lucky.

No one was harmed, but it was scary for a time. I remember the nervous laughter of that experience, especially when we were safely back on shore. Fortunately, they have hired me since. Or, on another occasion the swell was so high that we just kept rising and rising. It felt as though we were three stories above the surface. And, we were. It too was frightening, but we made it back safe – another "Dear God" moment.

Like I said, you rarely learn from things that always go right. Sometimes you have to experience brushes with danger, things that go wrong, bad judgment calls, not following your checklist, and renegade weather – to learn your lesson. You are certain to have something go amiss: lose an anchor, return back late in dark, forget water, make a poor landing, and even hit bottom at some point. It is important to instill the fear that it takes to keep you safe. It will hopefully prevent unwelcome scenarios, the likes of:

> "Dear God, if you help me get out of this nightmare situation, I promise not to make this mistake ever again. It was stupid of me, I know. I knew better. But, here I am. And, I am scared. All I ask is that you help me this one time. I'll even go to church if you do – that's a promise. Please God, I need this. Thank you."

But, you do. You will make this mistake again. And, you will ask God a favor at least a few more times in your boating life – whether you believe in him or her, or not – even if you didn't go to church.

On that note, you now have the tools that you need to boat safely and proficiently. Never get over confident. Just be confident enough and know where to go. Safe, smart, and decisive – with caution, common sense, and consideration of others. Happy boating!

KNOTS

Knots are a very important in boating and boating safety. Knowing how to tie a bowline, cleat hitch and clove hitch are a must.

BOWLINE

One of the most useful knots you can know. The Bowline forms a secure loop that will not jam and is easy to tie and untie. The Bowline is most commonly used for forming a fixed loop, large or small at the end of a line.

CLEAT HITCH

The Cleat Hitch is the best way to tie a boat to a dock. It is a quick and easy method of tying a rope to a cleat on a dock or boat that is also easy to untie.

CLOVE HITCH

A simple all-purpose hitch. Easy to tie and untie. A useful and easy to tie knot, the Clove Hitch is a good binding knot. A half hitch can be added to secure the clove hitch.

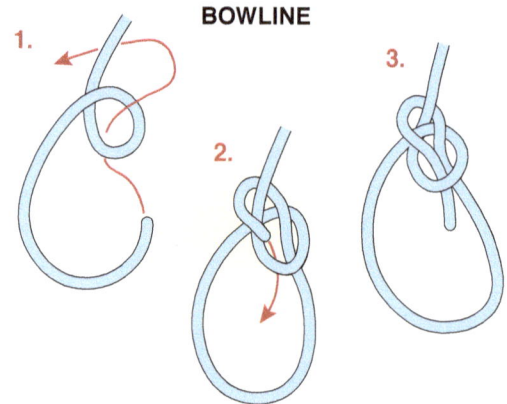

BOWLINE

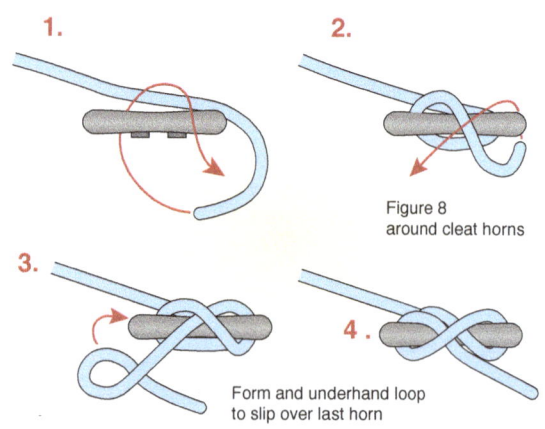

CLEAT HITCH

Figure 8 around cleat horns

Form and underhand loop to slip over last horn

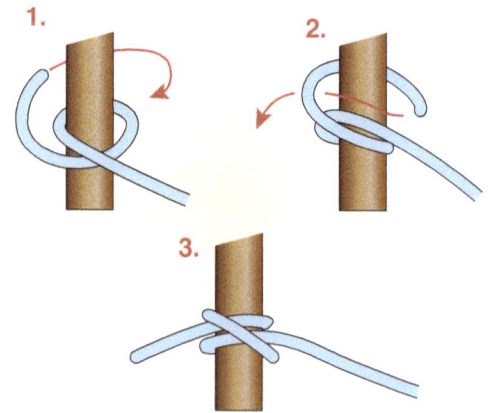

CLOVE HITCH

FIGURE EIGHT

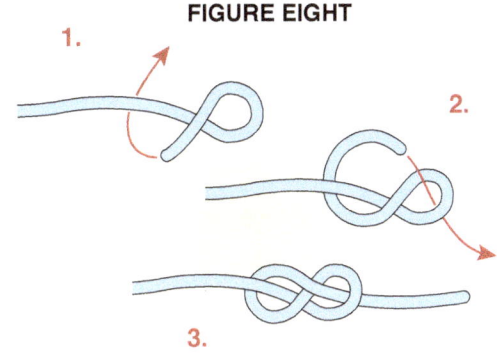

FIGURE EIGHT

The Figure Eight Knot is a stopper knot that helps in sailing by not allowing the tag end of a rope to slip out of it's retaining device, or pulley.

TRUCKER'S HITCH

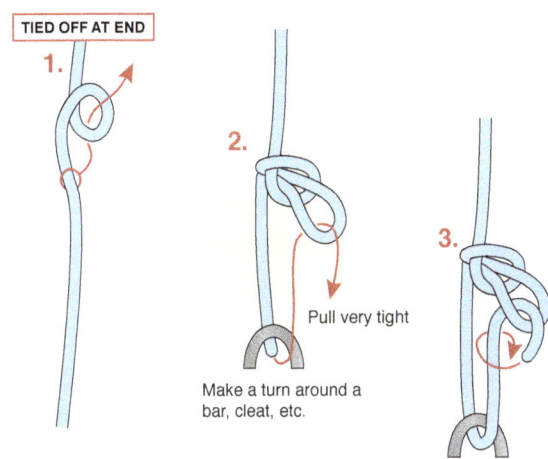

TRUCKER'S HITCH

Use the Trucker's Hitch to cinch down a load. This combination of knots allows a line to be pulled very tight. It is used by truckers to secure heavy loads in place and works equally well tying kayaks to the tops of cars. Once the line is pulled to the desired tension using the pulley effect, the knot is secured with two half hitches around one or both lines.

HALF HITCH

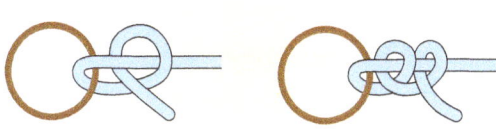

Single Half Hitch   Two Half Hitches

HALF HITCH

Two half hitches can be used to tie a rope to a tree, boat or any object. It is often used in a supporting role, for example to increase the security of a primary knot.

Q & A

BOATING Q&A

This is not a quiz, but it could be. Instead, it's a review, and another way for me to answer a lot of your questions.

1. **What does 4-C's stand for?**
   Caution, Common sense, Consideration of others and Communication - in boating and in life.
2. **What 4 apps do you check prior to getting on the water?**
   1. Weather, 2. Windfinder, 3. MyRadar, and 4. Tides4Fishing.
3. **What is a shoal?**
   Shallow water, or a sandbar just below the surface.
4. **Name four important checklist items.**
   1. To have all USCG required gear, 2. Drinking water, 3. Fuel, and 4. Cell phone.
5. **What is a float plan?**
   A notice that you leave with someone on shore re: your route and expected return time. Call in or text if it should change.
6. **What should you mention to your passengers prior to getting on plane?**
   "We're about to go fast. Is everyone ready?"
   PS: make sure that motor is lowered all the way and aligned straight, that nothing can fly away, rid throttle play, then "punch it" or get on plane, ...and after, taper off some.
7. **What is the AAA of boating?**
   TowBoatUS, Sea Tow, or insurance with tow coverage.
8. **Name two things to remember prior to launching your boat from a trailer.**
   1. Put the plug in, and 2. Take the aft straps off.
9. **Name five USCG required items**
   1. Life jackets, 2. Flares, 3. Horn, 4. Throw cushion, and 5. Type B fire extinguisher.
10. **Name one more USCG required item?**
    Your original boat registration (in a plastic zip lock bag). A waterproof box is a good idea too.
11. **Name three additional (non required) safety items to have on board.**
    1. First aid kit, 2. Throw line with buoy, and 3. Sunscreen.

12. **Name two main priorities associated with driving a boat.**
    1. Depth 2. Awareness of surroundings: other boats, trap buoys, debris, and marine life.
13. **What do you check on an outboard motor before you leave the dock?**
    That the tracer (or cooling water) is streaming out of the motor.
14. **What is your boating playground?**
    The four or five places in your area that you get to know intimately (in all conditions) so that your boat outings are consistently fun, safe, and incident free.
15. **What is a common procedure for docking?**
    Approach 90° in forward idle, turn at one boat length away, then neutral / walk the bow over by turning all the way toward the dock. Next, walk the stern over in reverse, then neutral.
16. **Name three ways to approach / pass over waves**
    1. Slowly approach head on (for large boat wakes), 2. Slow down some at waves, pass, then accelerate, and 3. Slow down and turn as you arrive at wave (aka hip check), then accelerate and ride peaks and valleys of other boat's wake.
17. **What should you always do prior to turning or stopping?**
    Look around (side to side and behind you) for other boats.
18. **How do you "tell" your boat what to do?**
    Thrust the motor some (in control) so that it growls and thus turns (often used in windy conditions and 3-point turns).
19. **What should you do if you hit a lobster pot buoy?**
    Turn motor off, Raise motor and assess. Have knife, mask and snorkel on board. If need be, put dive flag up and anchor.
20. **Name Four factors when dropping an anchor**
    1. Depth, 2. Current, 3. Boat direction, and 4. Scope.
21. **Name five things associated with retrieving an anchor**
    1. Communication, 2. Hand signals, 3. Bird nesting, 4. Cleaning off anchor, and 5. Resetting zip tie.
22. **What should you do every time you anchor?**
    Disconnect the kill switch, because it helps you remember to bring in your ladder, lower your dive flag, bring in your chum, and secure your cushions, etc.

23. Name two other reasons for disconnecting the kill switch.

    1. It makes the boat child proof, and 2. It can help prevent unintended accidents.

24. What are the two anchor retrieving hand signals?

    1. Karate chop = forward and direction, and 2. Fist = neutral.

25. Name 3 things associated with man overboard readiness.

    1. Improvisation with gear on board, 2. Toss line / throw cushion, and 3. Do NOT dive in.

26. What do you do when you find yourself in a head on situation with another boat?

    Turn to starboard so to let the other boat know your intention.

27. Name 4 concerns associated with boats and bridges.

    1. Height of bridge vs. fishing rods / outriggers, 2. Channel lights 3. People fishing from road above, and 4. Current.

28. What are two most common scope ratios in anchoring?

    1. 5:1, and 2. If stronger current, 7:1. If overnight or in a squall, maybe 10:1 and two anchors.

29. Name three things associated with a GPS.

    1. Depths, 2. Tracks, and 3. Coordinates

30. Name 4 other GPS advantages.

    1. Tide information (on some), 2. Speed indicator, and 3. Sonar and 4. Water temperature.

31. What do you do when you get on the water, but feel uncomfortable with the conditions?

    1. If choppy only on, e.g., ocean side, try the bay side instead. 2. Return to dock / home, and live to boat another day.

32. What distance should keep from a diver down flag?

    100 is the magic number: 100 yards in open water, and 100 feet (when possible) in narrow channels at idle speed.

33. What three knots should you be well acquainted with?

    1. Bowline, 2. Clove hitch, and 3. Cleat knot. Other knots: Trucker's hitch, Half hitch, Figure 8. See page 82.

34. How do you get a stuck anchor out?

    Tie the anchor line off to a port / starboard cleat, slowly drive 30 degrees off the anchor line, drive 3 to 5 mph, until free.

35. Name things to look for beside boats and marine life.

    Plastic bags, cans, and styrofoam. Please pick up, secure, and dispose of on land. Thank you!

36. How do you know if your anchor is dragging?
    1. You are farther from your anchor indicator, buoy or other.
    2. The boat is sideways to the anchor.
37. How should one communicate on a boat?
    Make sure that your mouth is facing in the direction of who it is you are talking to.
38. How do you prevent the anchor line from hurting your hands when in a strong current?
    Let out line (and slack) so you can "take a wrap or bight" around the cleat without catching your fingers.
39. How often should you check weather, radar and wind?
    Every two hours is a good rule of thumb, and visually (for storms on the horizon) too.
40. Name 3 reasons to use your trim tabs
    1. To level out the boat side to side due to passenger weight, 2. To raise weather side so to keep passengers dry, and 3. Trim tabs also help some boats get on plane faster.
41. Name 3 reasons to trim your motor up.
    1. To help lift the bow some (if too much weight in bow), 2. To protect the prop / lower unit when going through "skinny" water while on plane, and 3. To protect the seagrass when maneuvering into or out of shallow water.
42. What advisable action should you take when caught in a sudden storm or squall?
    Hunker down, lower an anchor or two with maximum scope, stay low, and wait for weather to pass
43. Who is right, your gut instinct or your GPS?
    In most cases the correct answer is your GPS, especially for shoal locations and markers.
44. What are those white and sometimes colored styrofoam balls floating in the water?
    These are lobster or crab pot buoys. There is a long line between the buoy and trap below. It is important to be aware of incoming or outgoing tide for which side to pass them.
45. What do yellow spheres represent?
    Yellow balls / spheres represent a SPA zone, or Sanctuary Preservation Area, such as Looe Key. There are four spheres in the shape of a rectangle. No anchoring, fishing, standing

on, or touching is permissible. These are observe and enjoy (only) zones. Check out www.sanctuaries.noaa.gov.

46. **What is a tidal coefficient?**
    It is the amount of water moving from one tide to another that determines how strong the current is in a given place. A 50 tidal coefficient is average, whereas, a value of 100 is very strong and might cause your anchor to drag. Tidal coefficient is included on some online tide charts, like Tides4Fishing.

47. **What is a minus tide?**
    Charts and GPS numbers indicate depth at mean low tide. When a minus tide occurs, often around full moon but on other occasions too, the tide is less than what is says on a chart, sometimes one foot less. The opposite of minus tide, at high tide, is a king tide.

48. **What should I look for when buying a used boat?**
    It takes minutes to do a compression test. Take out all the spark plugs and test each cylinder one at a time. Go to YouTube to see how it's done. They should all be consistent, in the area of 135, or so, within 5 to 10 pounds of each other.

49. **Is there a big difference in having two outboards vs. one?**
    The biggest difference with twin outboards versus a single one, is threefold. 1. It is always better to have two motors than one when 25+ miles offshore, 2. Twin outboards have the ability to steer without using the wheel, and are commonly used as such when docking, or turning in a tight circle, and 3. On the plus side, you have more power. On the minus side, twice the maintenance and cost. I go with the plus – as long as you can afford it, and can take care of it.

50. **Do you recommend that I buy a Bulls Bay boat?**
    My Bulls Bay has served me well. It was within my budget. Buy what you can afford. I recommend a fairly new / used boat that has a motor(s) with low hours, and still under warranty. Definitely have it checked out: compression, hours, transom, electrical, soft spots, etc. There are some pretty great deals out there. You might even find a $40K boat for $20K.

51. **Bonus Question: Where can I find a hands-on boating lesson in the Florida Keys – with a place to stay?**
    Keys Boat Tours and Captain Brian – 305-699-7166

YOU: TRIM IT, TACK IT & SAIL IT

Sailing is not as difficult to learn, as convincing yourself that sailing is not that difficult. This is the first hurdle to clear. To begin, find the wind. Put your face in the direction of the wind. Do you feel it on both ears? Where is it coming from – east, south? Pay attention to its direction at all times. It can change, and does. Next up: a judgment call. Is the wind too strong for your boat? Is it too light and not worth the effort to set the boat up? Or, is it just right? Is it going to get stronger or weaker? What is the forecast? You know the answer to this because you checked the weather, wind, and tide charts beforehand. You went online and checked *forecast.weather.gov* and **MyRadar** app. You know the wind conditions because you visited *Windfinder.com*. And, you know the tides because you went to, *Tides4Fishing.com*, or the app **Tides Near Me**. This information will tell you about the three most important factors in sailing. You need to know the weather in case any potential storms are on the horizon. You need to know the wind because – well, we are sailing. And, you want to know the tides, because it helps you with depth information and currents. Motor boating and sailing are very different, but much alike, in that they both take you a world away.

IN THE BEGINNING

Sailing is almost as old as man. Think of the discoveries made, the characters played; Columbus, Cortez, and Blackbeard to name a few; battles fought, flora and fauna, life and limb transported – shipwrecks. The stories are imbedded in our psyche. Sailing takes little more than an understanding of wind direction and how to use it to your advantage. The sail itself is both ingenious and very basic. Sailing offers adventure free of charge – and adventure awaits.

The goal of this lesson is to achieve understanding of sailing by practice: raising the sail, trimming, port and starboard tacks. From close hauled to running, raising and lowering the bilgeboards, tacking, jibes, anchoring, lowering and securing the sail, and even operation of the outboard motor. We hope to get you to a place where you can confidently and safely get on the water on your own, and perhaps even show a friend or a loved one – the joys of sailing.

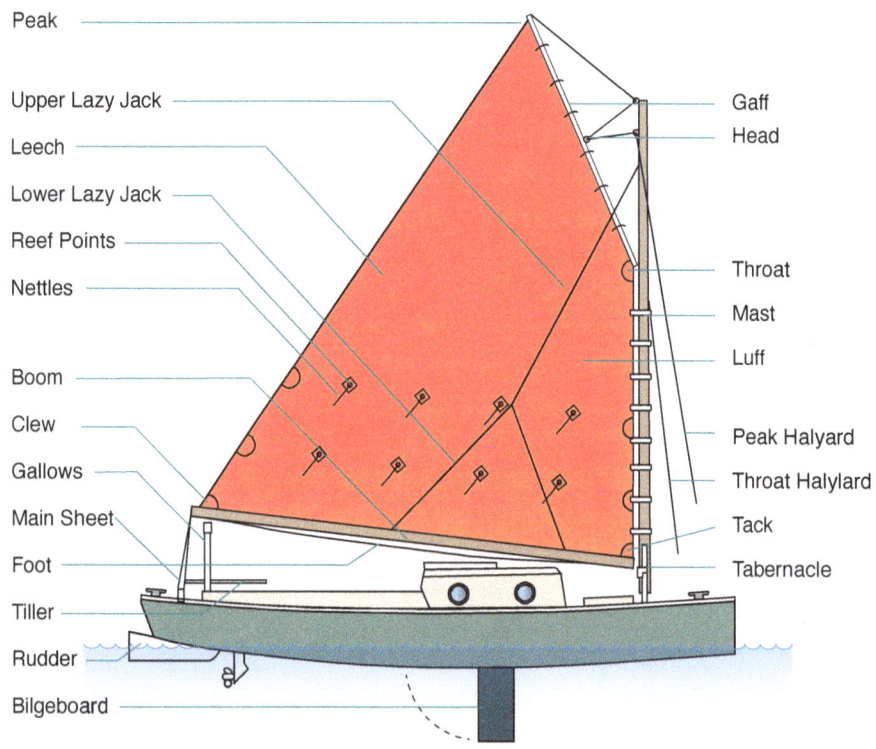

There are many components to sailing: wind direction, current, sail adjustment, and making sound judgment calls. This lesson hopes to make sense of it all – and to have fun. There is no better place to start than at the beginning. The boat we are learning on is simple yet more than sufficient. It is a gaff rigged cat boat design. It is a

slow boat performance wise, but very able enjoyment wise. It is a 21' Nimble Bayhen; a shoal draft flat bottom boat that uses bilgeboards rather than a ballast based centerboard or keel. Bilgeboards are similar to leeboards but fit into compartments inside of the cabin, rather than attach to the exterior sides of the boat.

The boat's design has a specific purpose much as all sailboats do. This boat, which we call **Why Knot?**, is specifically designed for shallow water. It is a bay boat, built in Florida to sail on the Florida Bay. The bilgeboards allow us to get into shallow water. The main purpose of a bilgeboard, leeboard, centerboard, and keel is the same – to keep the boat from being pushed sideways. This underwater resistance enables the boat to make headway, rather than side-way. A centerboard and keel offer the bonus of stability, and heeling capability, because they are weighted with lead ballast.

YOU: TRIM IT, TACK IT & SAIL IT   93

COMPONENTS

All boats, motor or sail, have a port side, starboard side, bow and stern. All sailboats have a mast, boom, rudder, and helm – in our case, a tiller. Some masts are supported side to side and front back with cables that comprise of stays, shrouds, and turnbuckles. The boat that we are on – does not. It has a free standing mast mounted in a tabernacle with a pivot point. The mast is designed to pivot down when the need occurs, whether to trailer, or to pass under a bridge. This is especially convenient in Keys waters with its many low bridges. Ropes on sail boats are known as halyards, sheets, and lines. The halyard is the rope that raises the sail. On a gaff rigged sailboat, there are two halyards: one for the peak, and another for the throat. The peak  is the outer top part of the sail, while the throat hugs the mast. The hoops connecting the sail to the mast are called mast hoops. We raise the sail in unison, looking up to watch for balance. The peak, or top/aft mechanism, should always stay ahead of the throat.

CAST OFF

Let's motor out to a safe spot. This is the opportune time to practice steering – before we sail. When the sail is up there are many working parts: sheet, cleat, bilgeboard, mainsail and wind – a lot is going on. Learning how to steer with a tiller can be counter intuitive at first. Let's motor around until you get the hang of it. Next, we will lower the anchor so that the boat is pointing into the wind. It is only then that you can raise the sail. You want to position the boat into the wind prior to anchoring. A way to raise the sail without anchor-

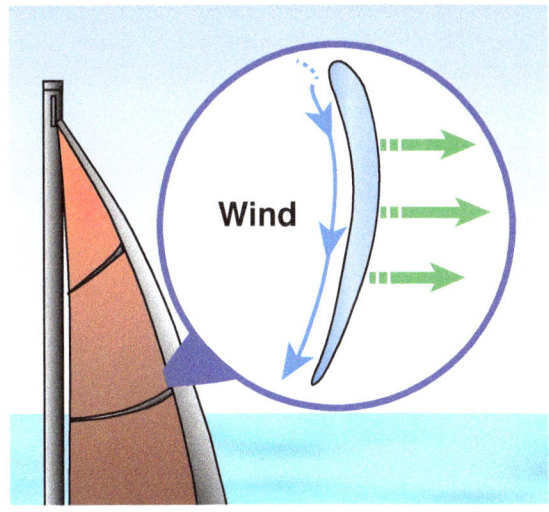

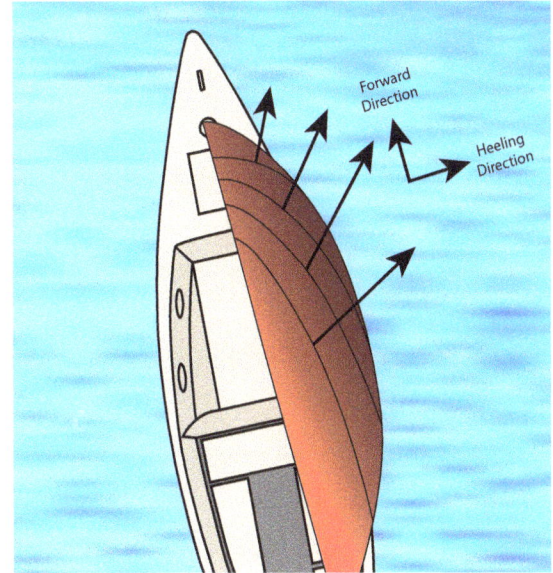

ing, is to have one person motor and steer into the wind while the other person raises the sail, even if a bit of a battle.

The rope that operates the main sail is known as the mainsheet. All sailboats have a mainsail. Many other sailboats also have a jib, a sail forward of the mainsail. **Chapman Piloting & Seamanship** is a very thorough reference book that discusses the many different sailboat designs.

The part of the boat that lies along the bottom of the sail is known as the boom. I am not certain if it got its name through unfortunate circumstances, from hitting so many people in the head, but it's definitely a good way to remember – so to not let the boom hit you in the head. Others say it was derived from the Dutch word for tree, "boom". In any case, the sail is our motor. It propels the boat forward. If you look at a sail from the front, you will see that it is shaped similar to an airplane wing, but vertical. Both airplanes and sailboats operate under the same principle, **Bernoulli's Law**, factoring air molecules. Air molecules move faster on one side of the sail / wing than the other, creating lift. We trim the sail according to different points of sail.

POINTS OF SAIL

We would still move forward without bilgeboards, but we would also get pushed sideways. We still move sideways some with the bilgeboard lowered, but not nearly as much as without. So, we trim the sail according to the desired direction we go, or tack. We also adjust the bilgeboard according to our point of sail or heading.

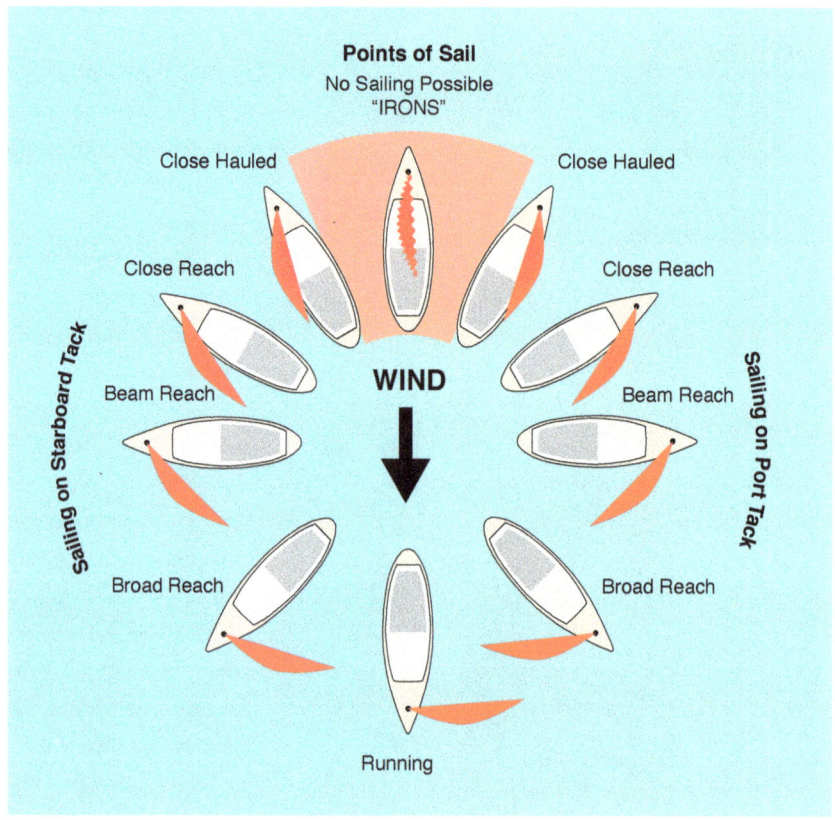

We rely most on the bilgeboard when we are close to the wind, heading up or into the wind. As the boat moves away from the wind, we rely less on the bilgeboard. If the wind is directly behind us, we don't need the bilgeboard at all because there is no force pushing the boat sideways. Different tacks include close hauled, beam reach, broad reach, and running with the wind. The bow of the boat moves from 12 o'clock to 6 o'clock on either side, as shown above with port and starboard tacks. When close hauled, heading as high into the wind as possible but still making headway, the sail needs

to be trimmed all the way in, with the boom nearest to the cockpit. As we move away from the wind, we ease out the sail some. When the wind is perpendicular to the boat, coming from the side, the sail is eased out 1/3 of the way. When the wind is just aft of the starboard beam, the sail is 3/4 out. When the wind is directly behind us, the sail is 90 degrees to the boat. But, it is very important that the wind stays on one side the boat, port or starboard, so that we do not jibe. That is to say, we need to maintain a definitive starboard tack or port tack. If on a starboard tack, and wind coming over starboard hind quarter, we have to be sure to keep the wind over the starboard side, and not allow it to pass over to the port side. Otherwise, the result could be an uncontrolled jibe, where the boom flies across the boat unintentionally. Uncontrolled jibes can lead to injury – and even capsize. "Trim the sails" means to adjust the sail in or out so that it has the correct amount of wind, not overpowering, and not luffing. Instead, the sail is perfectly shaped, or full.

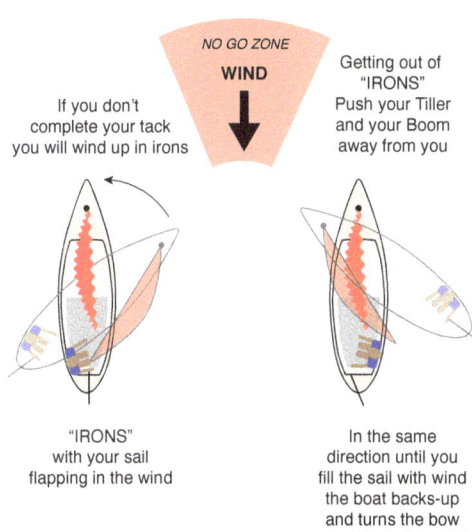

YOU: TRIM IT, TACK IT & SAIL IT   97

"Ease out" means to let the sail out some. "Head up" means to move closer into the wind. "Fall off" means to move away from the wind. When your bow is approximately 45° off the wind, you are "close hauled." When you steer the boat to leeward, or away from the wind, you are "falling off." If your sailboat points directly into the wind, you are in "irons," or stopped.

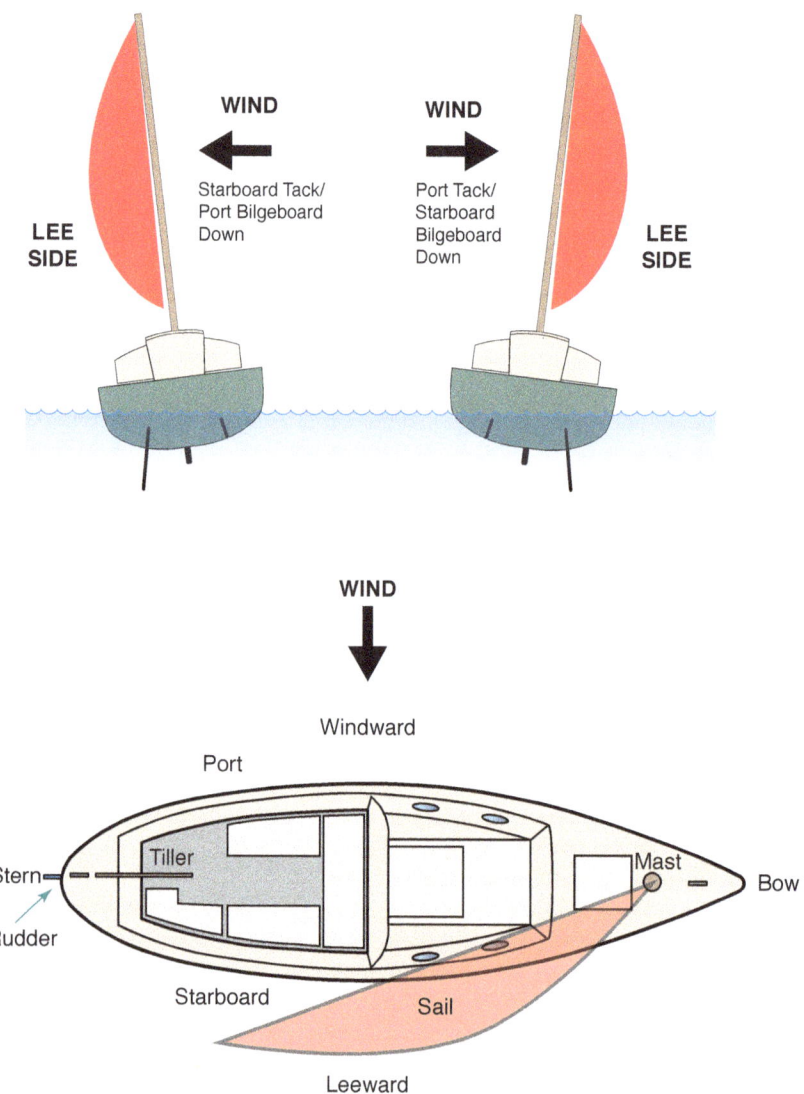

PORT AND STARBOARD

As previously mentioned, sailing is divided into two halves that mirror one another. The same rules apply on each side. Whatever your tack, port or starboard, the bilgeboard on the lee side is the one to operate. The best way to remember which bilgeboard should be down (because you only use one at a time), is to think

of a bilgeboard as a leeboard, and always lower the lee side board, opposite the direction of the wind. When on a starboard tack, the wind is coming over the starboard side. In this instance, you would lower the port side (or lee side) bilgeboard. When you turn around, or go from a starboard tack to a port tack, the bow has crossed the wind. Raise the port side bilgeboard and lower the starboard bilgeboard. You have just gone from a starboard tack to a port tack. The windward side board is always raised, and the leeward bilgeboard is the one in use, or lowered.

There is the deck of the boat, cockpit, helm, wheel or tiller. There are gunwales, freeboard, hull, chine, and bottom. There are toe rails, handholds, cleats, pulleys and chocks. Sail parts include foot, leech, luff, clew, tack, and head. We "flake" the sail when we lower it, and we use bungees to keep the sail from blowing around. We have an out-haul and a down-haul. Some sails, like ours, even have battens as sail stiffeners. There is the cabin, hatches, and portholes. We have an outboard motor. And, we also have oars and oarlocks.

The anchor line is called the "anchor rode." The "bitter end" of the anchor rode is attached to the mast. The anchor is attached to a shackle, chain, and the rode. Ours is a Bruce anchor, or plow anchor. We also have a Danforth anchor. We will practice anchoring and scope, or the amount of rope we let out for the given depth. The rule of thumb is generally 5:1. If it is five feet deep, we let out twenty-five feet of rode. The stronger the wind or current, the more scope. It is at this point that we cleat the anchor.

OUR BOAT

One great feature to this boat is the mainsheet. It is the same rope that controls the mainsail regardless of whether you are on a port tack or starboard tack. A jib sail often has independent sheets for port and starboard tacks. Our mainsheet utilizes a cam cleat, used to lock the mainsheet in place, rather than having to hold onto it. It offers the ability to be hands free during long tacks. As we adjust the sail, we simply disengage the cam cleat, and "sheet in" or "sheet out." Still, lines do get fouled on occasion, so it is important to keep everything "shipshape" and not "three sheets to the wind" – or disorganized.

There are compartments under the seats in the cockpit area. This is where we keep our life jackets, flares, horn, dry box, first aid kit, tools, spare line, and handheld bilge pump. There is also a battery and 12V charger. We have a chart, basic navigation tools, a swim ladder, reef safe sunscreen, fins, mask, and extra drinking water.

We keep spare fuel in the open air under the bench seat. You want to be prepared for most anything. So, we have a dry bag with a change of clothes. We also let someone on land know where we are, and what time we expect to return, our float plan.

READY ABOUT?

It is now time to practice, "coming about." It means crossing the wind with your bow, and changing your tack, be it starboard to port or port to starboard. We do this repeatedly until we have the language down and the practice perfected. *"Ready about?"* the helmsperson calls. *"Ready!"* the crew responds, *"Hard to lee,"* the helmsperson hails, as s/he pushes the tiller all the way to the lee side, or away from self, so that the bow of the boat will cross the wind. It is a dance perfectly timed between helmsperson and crew, or captain and first mate. The helmsperson will steer the boat and adjust the mainsail while the mate lifts one bilgeboard and lowers the other. The wind has crossed to the other side, so too must the bilgeboard, but not premature – just right. Before we tack or jibe, as with all boating, we make sure that no other boats are too close. We have made our first tack, or our first turn. With each tack the goal is to find an efficient heading, so to maximize our ever blissful forward progress.

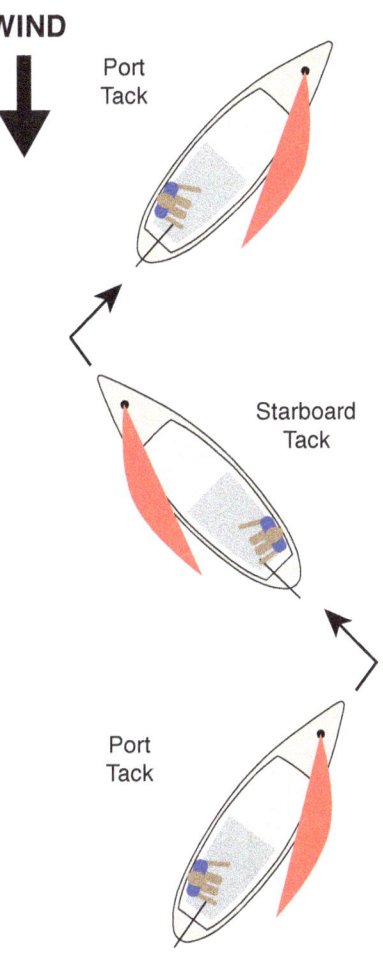

TERMINOLOGY

Head up, fall off, ease out, and sheet in - all terminology used when sailing. The one command that you don't want to hear, is *"Jibe ho"* unless done so intentionally. Coming about is when your bow crosses the wind. A jibe is when your stern crosses the wind. The whole purpose of any boating lesson is communication. We use specific terms for clear communication. Rather than point and say, *"watch out,"* everything needs to be cautious and precise, e.g., *"There is a buoy ahead of us to starboard."* We want our day on the water to be enjoyable, not stressful. We need to be smart and cautious and conscious of our surroundings at all times – so to have fun.

Let's review; We motored from the marina to a good anchor spot. We anchored and tied off to a cleat. We raised the sail. We are shipshape. There are times at anchor, when you have to back the sail into the wind, push toward the wind, so to fall off into a port or starboard tack. Otherwise, you are just stuck – in irons. One person lifts the anchor and the helmsperson falls off, but only after looking around for other boats. We need to remain careful, mindful, and observant at all times, while at the same time, enjoy the moment.

We are on a starboard tack. The wind is coming over the starboard or windward side of the boat. The bilgeboard on the lee / port side is down. The bilgeboard on the windward side is up. If this were a centerboard, it is always down except when you are running with the wind, aka heading down wind – the wind is behind you. That said, the centerboard does adjust up and down for different points of sail. It is important that we know where the wind is coming from. It is important also, to be careful near bridges and overhead cables. We are always aware of the depth, and mindful of all things GPS.

RUN AGROUND?

In the event that we ever run aground, because we travel in shallow water, we have a plan in place. Step 1) drop the sail, Step 2) lower the anchor, Step 3) assess the situation. Step 4) have wet shoes accessible (to get out and push), or Step 5) use the oars, Step 6) drink water, Step 7) lower the anchor again and reset the sails. Alternate Step 7) If it's getting dark, the tide is falling, and you are still stuck, it is time to call home, or perhaps **TowBoatUS** or **Sea Tow** for rescue = common sense / judgment call. Aren't you glad that you have a membership with one of these services? Boating doesn't always go right. In fact, it can often go wrong. *Note: Most recreational boaters do not wear life jackets, but I recommend that you do, if only a Type 3 PFD, personal flotation* device. It just might save your life.

In most every stressful situation, it is how you deal with it that counts. I experienced a situation where I anchored the boat and raised the sail, hoping that it would luff as it should when pointed into the wind. What happened instead however, the mainsheet got snagged in the cam cleat, so we were in effect sailing while at anchor. The danger here is dragging your anchor, and the very real possibility of an out of control jibe. It is important to keep in practice, learn from mistakes and know your equipment. It turned out that my mainsheet line was a little too thick for the cam pulley. I didn't want to spend another $100 for a thinner mainsheet, but that's what I ended up doing. Better safe than sorry. There are too many bad boating stories out there. Things happen; anchors break loose, boats hit each other, people slip and fall, and equipment fails from time to time. You have to take the time to learn – and to always be careful.

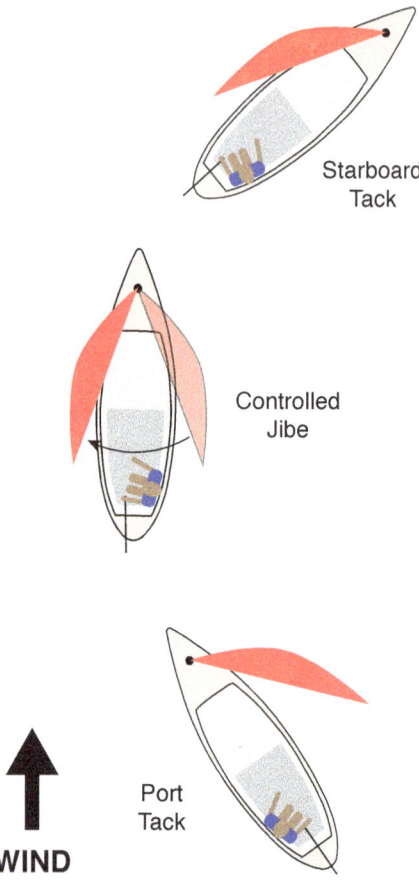

JIBE HO

We are getting the hang of this sailing thing: starboard tack, port tack, bilgeboard shift, and terminology. It's all coming together. I'd say it's about time for jibe practice. Rather than "hard to lee" and crossing the wind with the bow, we pull the tiller to windward, so to allow the back of the boat / stern to cross the wind. But, before we do, we look for other boats. We also pull the mainsheet all the way in so that the boom is centered on the cockpit. *"Prepare to jibe,"* the helmsperson orders. *"Ready,"* the crew responds. *"Jibe ho,"* the helmsperson commands. As the wind crosses to the other side, the helmsperson starts to ease out the sail, because rather than close to the wind after this maneuver, like when we come about, the boat is now far off the wind. The sail needs to ease out perhaps halfway before being trimmed back in to the desired tack, e.g., close hauled, beam reach, or broad reach – depending on your desired tack.

PRACTICE MAKES PERFECT

There is a lot to remember in sailing; wind direction and keeping track of it is difficult for some people. When to sheet in and sheet out is another learning curve. Terminology alone can be a stumbling block for many. How do we protect from a jibe? Or, execute a controlled jibe? How does one read the wind, or see a gust or puff of air coming? How should one react to said scenario? How do we stop for a swim? How do we get underway again? These are all things that you might do in a normal day of sailing. We will take it one subject at a time: wind, points of sail, adjusting the sail or "trimming", and reading the wind. Like anything else, practice makes perfect. Sailing is a language all its own that can only be learned by doing. It is possible for you to learn to sail at home without visiting the FL Keys, be it at the Key West Sailing Academy or Seacamp, but what an excuse to do so. In the event that you cannot slip away, I recommend that you use this lesson and find someone to teach you.

IN CONCLUSION

It is easiest to learn sailing on a small sailboat, if only to get the hang of wind direction, tacking, jibing, and maybe even capsizing. Similar to motor boating, some people get it quicker than others. Sometimes it is trial by fire. I once had a 46' gaff rigged sloop to use for a summer. Some friends of mine and I sailed her out into the Atlantic Ocean, but we arrived to our destination in the dark and had a near miss with a jetty. It was a harrowing experience, one that I will never forget. But, we were able to adjust / tack in time and live to tell about it. These are teaching moments – life lessons too.

Some might say that there are two types of people, sailing people and motor boat people. It is not entirely unlike dog people and cat people. It usually depends how you were brought up, or what you were first introduced to. I am both. I like sailing and motor boating. I also like dogs and cats – even though I was a dog person first.

My experience at Outward Bound, an outdoor adventure leadership school, taught me a lot. I started as a student and then became an assistant instructor for three years. It is important to challenge yourself: to learn, try, fail, and ultimately – succeed. But, few rarely master. Anyway, it is not really the point, for we will always keep learning, or never stop learning.

Motor boating and sailing is comparative to driving a car and riding a bicycle. Sailing is quieter and offers more time to take things in. Sailing is also slower and indirect. It is not necessarily easier, especially if you are confronted by what mother nature can throw at you. But, there is something liberating about being powered by wind. You don't have to use a motor – ever. Or, mostly never, but we have the option. Outward Bound boats don't use a motor, and they stay out for weeks at a time. If it is adventure you seek – sail.

My follow-up book to this one, **Navigating The Florida Keys And Finding Yourself** is about just that – adventure, perspective check, appreciation, and taking the time to let it all soak in; a 5-day journey sailing through the backcountry of the FL Keys, from Bahia Honda to Key West.

Many people tell me, *"I have always wanted to learn how to sail."* Now is your opportunity to do so. This lesson, like our motor boat and fishing lesson, is transferrable to where you live. An experienced sailor at your marina or neighborhood can follow along and show you. Granted, it is not as specific as the 3-hour motor boat lesson. Sailing has to be learned by doing. Like life, you are either at the helm or a passenger. The decision is up to you. But, sailing offers a great opportunity, even as metaphor – to take the helm, call the orders, demand efficiency, take responsibility, and be a leader. It also offers the opportunity to get away, enjoy the water, and be one with the wind – and nature.

I had a guy once invite me to go fishing. I said, *"Sure, that sounds great."* He then said, *"Well, you might change your mind when you're out there with me – I'm a screamer."* I said, *"You mean that you scream in delight when you catch a fish?"* He said, *"No, I scream at you if you don't do it the way I want you to."* I said, *"Oh, no thanks."* Believe it or not, there are screamers in sailing too, but those are usually limited to sailboat racing – the Dr. Jekyll and Mr. Hyde types, the autocratic captain who very well might be your friendly neighbor while ashore. Those are the sailboats you cannot wait to get off of. Our lesson is not for screamers – but it is for dreamers.

The hope is that you can take more out of this experience than a sailing lesson. Sometimes you have to be in the middle of nowhere to find yourself, to live your truth, to know your story. I am not saying that I can deliver on that part, but it is a good mindset. You might just come to learn how to sail. My hope is this: that in sailing and in life, your tacks are clean, your jibes are few, and that you make peace with the forces of nature – the things that you have no control over. The following **Q&A** is not a quiz but a review. If you have any additional questions, please don't hesitate to contact me, *info@keysboattours.com*. Happy sailing!

Q&A

SAILING Q&A

This is not a quiz, but it could be. Instead, it's a review. Learn these thirty **Q&A** and practice boating. You are certain to be a better sailor than most. Happy sailing!

1. What is a port tack?
   A port tack means that the wind is coming over the port side of the vessel, or the left side as you are looking toward the bow.

2. Which side of the boat is starboard?
   Starboard is the right side of the boat as you are looking toward the bow.

3. Define the difference between windward and leeward?
   Windward is the side that the wind is coming from. Leeward is the side that the wind is going to.

4. What does "Coming about" mean?
   Coming about means that you are going to turn into / and cross the wind with the front of your boat, or the bow.

5. What is a jibe?
   A jibe is when you carefully allow the stern (back) of your boat to pass from one side of the wind to the other, port to starboard, or starboard to port.

6. How does an uncontrolled jibe happen?
   An uncontrolled jibe generally happens when you lose sight of the wind direction, and allow the wind to pass from starboard to port, or port to starboard while running with the wind.

7. What does it mean if you are "In irons?"
   In irons means you are heading into the wind, and therefore cannot make progress. When raising a sail, it is intentional.

8. What do I mean when I say, "Head up?"
   Head up means to move closer to or / in the direction of the wind. The result is – close hauled, or e.g., 45° off the wind.

9. Which bilgeboard should be down on a starboard tack?
   It is always the opposite. If the wind is coming over the right side, or starboard, the left or port side / leeward bilgeboard should be lowered. Think of it as a leeboard, lee side down.

10. What is the mainsheet?
    The mainsheet is the line that controls the mainsail.

11. **What design rig sailboat has a peak and a throat?**
    There are many boats that have this set-up, but the rig design is – gaff rig.
12. **What is a beam reach?**
    A beam reach is when the wind is hitting you directly from the side, port or starboard – on the beam.
13. **What do I mean when I say, "Fall off?"**
    I am saying that you should move away from the wind or, fall off. Let it blow you away, or down. You also let the sail out.
14. **Which direction does the tiller move when the command is "Come about?"**
    The actual command is Ready about / Hard to lee. Which means that you should always move the tiller away from you, toward the lee side. This action places the bow into the wind.
15. **What first measures should be taken if you run aground in a sailboat?**
    In general, you should first lower the sail so that you stop sailing - especially when aground. Take power away.
16. **What is a broad reach?**
    A broad reach is when the wind comes over the back third of the vessel, whether on the port or starboard side. You are almost running with the wind, but not quite.
17. **Define close hauled?**
    Close hauled is when you are as close to the wind as possible, 45° off the wind. This, depending on the boat design.
18. **Which brings you closer to the wind, a jibe or a tack?**
    When you tack, or "come about," you cross the wind with your bow, you are doing so close hauled. A jibe leaves you as far from the wind as possible – behind you in fact.
19. **When do you most need a bilgeboard, centerboard, or keel – close hauled or running?**
    The keel, centerboard, and bilgeboards / leeboards are most relied upon while close hauled, or closer to the wind.
20. **How do you anchor in a sailboat?**
    When anchoring a sailboat, make certain that your bow is facing into the wind, in irons, and sails luffing. Set the anchor, then drop the sails. Be quick about it but efficient. Note: Make sure that the lines are not fouled, that all remains shipshape.

21. **How do you prepare to return to the marina in a sailboat?**

    It is the same as anchoring, but in this case, you go into irons, drop your sail, flake it, and gather it with bungees Then, start your outboard, pull the anchor, and motor in. If the motor doesn't start, anchor and re-assess.

22. **What do we mean when we use the term "Sheets?"**

    Sheets are lines that operate your sails.

23. **What does "Sheet in" mean?**

    Sheet in means to pull your sail in, so that the boom moves closer to the center of the boat. You are trying to get closer to the wind, or to stop your sail from luffing.

24. **What does "Three sheets to the wind" mean?**

    This is an old sailing term that many people believe to mean – drunk. But, in truth, it means that your lines are flailing, and that your vessel is not shipshape.

25. **What do I mean when I say, "Tack?"**

    Tack can mean the direction you are currently on. You tack each time that you turn, aka coming about. In that sense, tacking is the opposite of a jibe.

26. **What does "Trim your sails" mean?**

    Trim your sails is what happens when you sheet in. You are making them as efficient as possible, or luff free.

27. **If you are luffing, what is happening?**

    Luffing happens when your sail(s) is into the wind, in irons, and sloppy, or not trimmed properly.

28. **If you get turned around, how do you find the wind?**

    If you lose sense of the wind direction, find it with your face. Another way to find the wind on many sailboats, is by looking at your telltales – yarn tied to your shrouds. But, not on our boat, because we have no shrouds.

29. **What is your heading?**

    Heading is your current compass position.

30. **What is your course?**

    Your course is a birds eye view of your day sail or crossing on a given day or journey.

A venting tool is used to help reverse the effects of barotrauma, in this case, to an amberjack. There is a descending device too. All deep water anglers are required to carry one of these tools.

YOU: RIG IT, BAIT IT & CATCH IT

The entire marine world is a catch as catch can cycle. It is one giant food chain that ranges from the apex predator to – a fly. In every ecosystem where man meets animal, there is a license to kill, literally. But, in every case, it is licensed with guidelines and rules. Most people follow these rules. A few don't.

Man has hunted fish since the beginning of time. In a place like the Florida Keys, fishing and catching is an ironic way of life, in that it often involves – death. Fishing is as old as time and an economic engine. So, we accept the concept as culture and allow our most basic human instinct of hunt or be killed – to flourish. But, we do so responsibly because we know that it is our life's blood.

I can relate to people who don't believe in killing anything – no matter what. There is a place for this argument, but it is not what this chapter is about. This chapter is about harvesting fish, and catch and release equally. It is also about sustainable and ethical fishing, however brutal it may seem. It is a cruel world, survival of the fittest. One could easily argue that fish got the wrong end of the stick.

That said, fishing is not especially easy to figure out on your own. Some might even say that fishing is an enigma because there is so much to it. Then, there is catching. Catching fish takes practice and passion, and for many, years of experience. But, the sole intention for all of us who fish, whether to keep or release – is to catch.

The challenging part is to find the fish: the rocky bottom, the humps, and holes. There is time of day, current, cold fronts, and water temperature to factor in. Fishing requires patience, and an investment far beyond gear. The pastime of fishing takes a certain amount of preparation, know-how, time, physical work, and always, clean-up, both the boat and the fish. It can be exhausting. But, it can be exhilarating too. In short, people get hooked!

This Florida Keys recreational fishing chapter will focus on inshore, reef, and offshore fishing: at anchor, adrift, and trolling, including backcountry, and patch reefs. We will target a variety of fish to catch, or just to get on the water for a good time – and release. At the chapter's end, in **Tips and Targeting**, we address the tactic of catching specific species including yellowtail snapper, mangrove snapper, mutton snapper, grouper, speckled trout, mackerel, dolphinfish (mahi), tuna, tarpon, lobster, and more. This personalized Florida Keys fishing lesson is a one of a kind. And, none too soon.

The ultimate goal of this chapter is to deliver solid information for the novice, but also – a saltwater fishing lesson that the seasoned angler can appreciate. This lesson hopes to provide you with enough good information to turn your otherwise confounding fishing life around. Granted, there is a learning curve to fishing. Some get it quicker than others. Case in point, to date: I have used the wrong line, wrong test strength, wrong weight, wrong hook, wrong bait, and wrong approach to presenting said bait. I have gone at the wrong time, wrong tide, and to the wrong place. I have caught the wrong fish – the ones I never intended to catch, and, I learned from it. Fortunately, I have a great fish app on my phone, **Fish Rules**, to inform me about the fish I do catch, and the guidelines that apply. You can learn from a pro who knows the proper approach, and catches on every outing, and you will. But, you can also learn from my early mistakes. I am not going to let all of that hardship go to waste. I have finally found a way to put all of that misery to good use – right here.

THE MYSTERY OF IT ALL

Similar to boating, there are good fishing days and bad fishing days. There are natural forces that predict good and not so good conditions for fishing: barometer, moon phase, wind, and migration to name a few. What I hope to demystify here are the basics of fishing – to start with, what good equipment the novice to semi-experienced angler should purchase. There is a market for the novice angler that I believe to be overlooked. Many tackle shops talk to you as if you are supposed to know. But, let's face it, you don't know, and you're not supposed to know. And, you hate to admit it. There is a lot to saltwater fishing. So, we start at the beginning, with the goal to get you up to speed sooner than later. YouTube videos are a great assist during this initial phase of fishing – and after.

QUESTIONS ABOUND

The list of questions are long and the answers are often few. But, answer we will, as will YouTube. Should you use braided line or monofilament? What size length leader, hook, and weights should you use in different conditions? How do you tie wire to your leader, and when? How can you save money on ice, chum, and bait? What should you have in your tackle box? What artificials and when? What knots should you tie? What is the best bait for a given species? And, last but not least, where do you go to find the fish?

But, there is no last in fishing. Fishing is a pastime of *"...just one more,"* a never ending win or die trying day-in and day-out effort. These are the things that I discuss in this chapter, and answer in the **Q&A**, because these are the things that only a father tells his child. If not for a family connection or a fishing fanatic friend, few fishermen offer up fishing tips – until now.

We will show you all of the above, including some GPS waypoints. Now, when I say we, I mean my guide and me. In that regard, I play the role of you, novice. And, as novice, my guide's role is to help make a better angler out of me. But, first to secure said guide. This is my first big challenge. Finding the right guide is a lot like targeting fish. The plan being to find someone who will teach us to rig equipment, locate fish, present bait, and ultimately – catch. I use the same approach as if I were new to boating. I am going to hire a guide to show me, mentor me, and save (us) time – perhaps years.

This is no small effort, because I am a known guide in the area and highly rated on TripAdvisor. Other local guides understandably don't want to reveal their secrets to me, especially their spots. And, I can't tell a lie, i.e., pose as a customer, because it is unethical and would harm my otherwise good reputation. So, I will find a guide who will benefit as I do – one who is interested in the concept of teaching, and likes the idea of being featured in this book, chapter, and cover. That is what I am targeting, and that is who I hope to catch. Together, we will deliver comprehensive information that will relieve you, the reader, of your fishing frustrations. We hope to answer all of your questions about fishing, beginning with the most requested query of them all, *"What am I doing wrong?"*

The days of going out and not catching are behind you. The feeling of regret, thinking what you could have accomplished on land had you not wasted a day on the water is a thing of the past. You are going to hire a person as I have, who catches on every outing. And, in return, aside from paying them and leaving a nice tip, you are going to write a favorable review for him or her online. You want to find reliable spots. And, to learn about targeting different species. This book supplies the novice with an array of questions to ask your

Capt. Jimmy

guide. Because, lets face it, many of you are still at the, *"What questions should I ask?"* – phase. Fortunately, I was very successful in my effort. I was able to secure a renowned guide to mentor us.

For many of us it is long overdue, but never too late. For others, it is perfect timing, early and promising. For everyone, it is finally time to have some fun fishing. Introducing, **Captain Jimmy Gagliardini** and **High Caliber Sportfishing Charters**. Captain Jimmy is a seasoned captain and fishing guide. He is a mentor one could only hope for. Raised in the Florida Keys, Captain Jimmy has fished the world, from Cabo to the Bahamas and then some. He is solidly booked throughout the year, entertaining clients with consistent catching. He has worked out of **Bluegreen Vacations Hammocks at Marathon Resort** for many years, and he has many return customers too. Fitting me in and agreeing to do this is super appreciated.

High Caliber Sportfishing Charters is just that – high caliber. Captain Jimmy will not just win you over, he will wow you. He offers a wide variety of fishing charters, from backcountry fishing to reef, wreck, and offshore catching. I explained to Captain Jimmy my needs for the book and my goal to collaborate for a positive win win. He agreed to guide me, much as I do in the hands-on boating lesson. In short, the tips pages reveal fishing as Captain Jimmy does.

Captain Jimmy and I, went on several outings together. Each outing is chronicled in **Tips & Targeting** so that you too can learn how to target selected species – and catch. We include species, set-up, bait, tackle, and tactic. I want this lesson to encourage you to call Captain Jimmy and High Caliber Sportfishing Charters for an outing. That is to say, I want your Florida Keys fishing vacation fulfilled, and your bucket list dream realized. Contact Captain Jimmy and **High Caliber Sportfishing Charters**, *highcalibersportfishingcharters.com* and call or text 305-395-0915. If for recreational tours and lessons, you can contact me, Captain Brian and **Keys Boat Tours**, at *keysboattours.com*. You can call or text me at 305-699-7166.

It is equally important to us that you learn how to catch where you live. Captain Jimmy's approach will apply to a certain degree. Use our **Q&A** and basic outline to begin. Hire a guide to fish, or better yet, to teach you. It is a completely different mindset, not to cater to you, but to mentor you. Captain Jimmy offers this service on every charter. If you are interested to learn, he is more than happy to share his knowledge with you, one that aligns with the Blue Star program for sustainable fishing, *sanctuarybluestar.org*. This alone is worth the charter fee.

THE HOW TO OF WHERE

But, how does one find the fish? That indeed is the million dollar question. Fishing is difficult in part because before you even begin, you find yourself fishing for advice, and tips, and answers that always appear illusive. The list of: to get, to do, to bring, and to go is long. The question of, *"Should I just go to the fish market instead?"* often comes to mind. So, with that in mind, we focus on targeting just one species at a time, e.g., how to, yellowtail, porgy, or mahi. When someone asks *"What are you fishing for?"* I tell my clients that there is only one answer – *"to relax."*

So, don't yell at your snagged line, lost leader, or skunked day, because the whole purpose was to catch some relaxation, right? Granted, a day out fishing is better than any day in the office – a world away in fact. But, for most of us, fishing is divided into two categories: a good day, and a bad day. A good day of fishing and catching on the water is a huge gift, not unlike seeing a dolphin during a sunset tour, or being eye to eye with a goliath grouper during a snorkel trip. Let's not kid ourselves, taking people out and not catching is stressful, especially if people are paying good money.

Many factors and even theories come into play with catching fish. Early morning and night time are generally better than daytime. A west wind in particular is not as good for fishing here in the Keys. Full moon has a reputation for being tough on fishing too. But, sometimes it can be great – especially with wahoo. Opposing wind and current are terrible for reef fishing at anchor. A southerly wind will help bring Gulf Stream marine life closer in, but sediment too, which can be a good assist to disguise your line and bait. Of course, the early bird catches the fish. Less boats and more chum in a given area lead to more fish and a better chance of catch. You might wonder how old timers consistently catch fish, so you approach one or two at the filet table and ask for information. You might approach several seasoned anglers and ask for one fishing tip from each, *"Could I ask you to share one fishing tip with me?"* You could accumulate 50 great tips. Put it in your notes. Also, look to see where charter fishermen fish. In that regard, ask the seasoned angler if he can share any numbers with you, i.e., good fishing spots. It doesn't hurt to ask. You will want to accumulate lots of your own numbers. Also, check out Cmor mapping, Navionics Vision Plus, and C-Map Reveal for your sonar to see structure better.

STRUCTURE

Fish love any type of structure. Structure in most cases is the reef, a wreck, a coral head grass, and rocks. But, structure could also be a branch, a tree, a sunk boat, dock pilings, and debris. All the while, you scour the water surface for fish activity and birds in the air. Out, say in 200' to 700' while mahi fishing, it is birds and weed lines to look for. In, e.g., Hawk Channel patch reefs, 25' to 45', and close to the reef in 50' to 75', your sonar should read a bottom with peaks and valleys until you see something that resembles jagged hills, or a boulder – or a ball of fish. Figure out the drift with your GPS

tracks. Anchor so that your chum drifts back to where the fish are. You want to lure the fish off of the structure to your hook. Chum generally takes 15 to 20 minutes to produce a good bite – so be patient. You want to have a variety of bait too; live pilchards and pinfish are popular, as is live ballyhoo, and chunk pieces of dead bait.

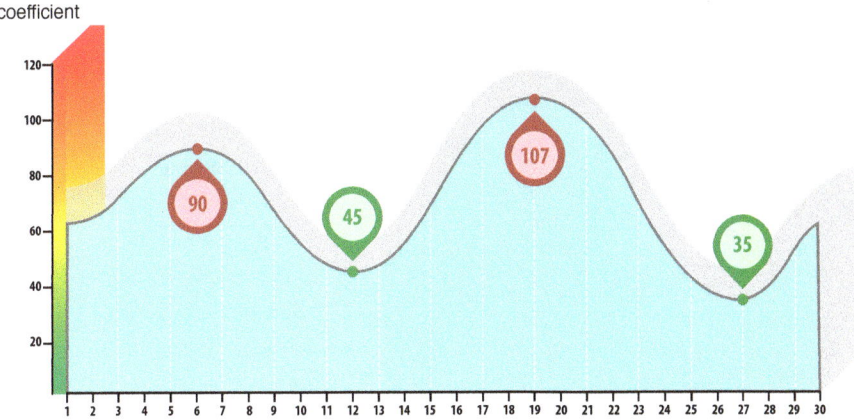

Tidal coefficients tell us the amplitude of the tide forecast (difference in height between the consecutive high tides and low tides in an area).

Some people fish for yellowtail only. Others, troll only. Many, who have no access to the water – bridge fish. Boaters can hit the patch reefs for mangrove snapper and grouper. Perhaps that fulfills you. Learn what time of year different fish migrate, and what the ideal water temperature is for said fish. Take notes: month, fish type, wind, tide, and water temperature. Then, record your positive results:

> 2/6/19, water temp 71, incoming tide, 10 am, limited out on big mangrove snapper under Bahia Honda Bridge in 1 hour
> - Amazing day!

Don't always take tide charts to heart. They are often inaccurate mainly due to tidal coefficient. When tidal coefficient is high, or the volume of water from one tide to the next is great – very high tide to very low tide, the predicted tide time can be delayed as much as two hours, especially at a bridge. It also makes for a very strong current, so be careful anchoring. You often want current, but there can be too much current too. You might fish when it is slack to rising, or perhaps an outgoing tide. Out near the reef, when a particular species isn't biting, you might target another. No current for yellowtail? So, head to the patch reef and bottom fish for mangrove snapper. Or, go to a wreck and drift for mutton and grouper. Jigging is a whole other style of fishing – and very physical. It too, takes practice. *Google: Vertical jigging with Captain Mike / YouTube.*

CHUM – YUM!

Aside from *"Go where the fish are"* advice, chum is perhaps the most overlooked basic of fishing. People tend to under chum, putting a 7 lb block into a fine mesh bag so to last longer. You need to attract the fish, and you do this by flaunting it – not skimping. Rather than a fine mesh bag, you want a 1"x1" wide mesh net, so that the chum flows. You can figure on a block or two of chum per hour. The next best tip is to streamline your presentation to one that is low profile. If yellowtailing, rather than start with a 20 lb leader and a 1/0 hook, try 10 lb leader and a #4 hook. It's okay if you don't know the lingo yet. My point is this: start smaller and leaner, with a presentation that mimics your chum, one that fish can't see as well.

SET-UPS

Your initial yellowtail set-up will be a 15 lb mono base line, and 10 lb leader. For mangrove snapper, it is a 12 lb leader on 20 lb base line mono. This, on a Penn 4500 spinning reel, and a light to medium action rod. If you are targeting 1 lb to 15 lb fish, lightweight rods are great fun. Have: 10 lb, 12 lb, 15 lb, and 20 lb+ fluorocarbon leader in your tackle box. Get a good assortment of hooks, weights, and jigs. I mainly use circle hooks. Hooks come in #1, #2, #3, and 1/0, 2/0, 3/0, and so on. The different sizes and types of hooks, is best understood here – *Google: Understanding fishing hooks / YouTube*.

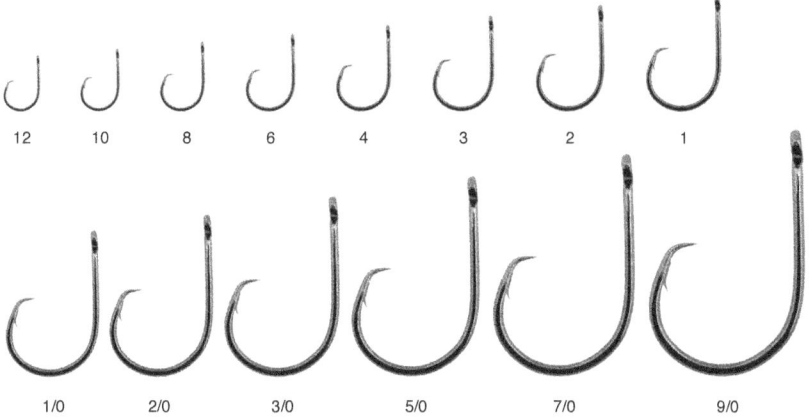

Hooks are classified by "sizes" – for example, a size 1 hook is larger than a size 6, while a 1/0 is smaller than a 7/0, pronounced *"7-aught."* The smallest standard sizes available are 32 and the largest 20/0.

You'd be surprised how effective a little hook is with catching a big fish. But, there are particular hooks that you will use when targeting particular species. For yellowtail, start with a #2 or #4 hook. If grouper or mutton snapper fishing, you will likely fish with a 4/0 to 7/0 circle hook. For mackerel, a #3 to #6 treble hook on wire.

You will learn the variety of hook designs from *YouTube: In-line circle hooks versus offset circle hooks, J hooks, long shank hooks, and so forth*. Here in the Keys, circle hooks are in most cases, the hook of choice. But, in the case of snapper fishing, it is not only choice – it is the law. A circle hook is designed to land in the corner of the fishes mouth. It prevents injury by keeping the fish from swallowing the hook. This is especially important during catch and release, or if the fish is not of legal size.

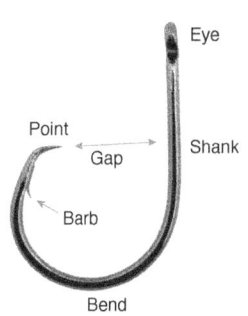

The top three priorities in fishing are: structure, chum, and presentation. Captain Jimmy will give you tips to locate the right spot, best prepare chum, and properly present bait. Picking the day is important too. Conditions vary, and boat size often plays a role.

Boating and fishing go hand in hand, so the **4-C's** rules still apply. There are days to go to the reef and other days to definitely not go, **Caution** = Keep close track of wind, radar and weather.
Common Sense = Never anchor too close to another angler.
Consideration = You are a better person for it. Of course,
Communication = Is key to all things understanding, and learning.

The use of center console boats here in the Keys is most popular. That, and an outboard motor or two. There are more outboard mechanics here, which is key. The limit for my 23' center console is 15 knots and 3' to 4' seas. And, at that, I will only go out when the 15 knot winds are coming out of the north – flatter seas. Why get beat up?

A 26' to 30' boat can head out in winds up to 20+ knots and 3' to 5' seas. But, if you are susceptible to motion sickness, even if you've never been sea sick before, there is always a first time, and these are those conditions. *Note: Best to take Dramamine the night before, and the morning of.* A center console boat allows you to walk around the helm, and has room for multiple anglers. The most popular length for an ocean going vessel is in the 30' range. This size boat and twin outboard motors allows you to go further out more safely. Two feet makes a big difference. The longer the boat, the smoother the ride, but also the more expensive to purchase, insure, fuel up, and maintain – all things to consider. The three basic styles of fishing that I discuss are: freelining, bottom fishing, and trolling. When yellowtail fishing, a #4 hook is freelined with nothing more than a bit of bait – bonito, shrimp, or minnows.

For mangrove snapper, we bottom fish using 4' of 12 lb leader, and depending on the current, a 1 oz to 5 oz egg sinker above the swivel. Then, a 2/0 to 4/0 circle hook with chunk ballyhoo or live pinfish. This is known as a Carolina rig. A Knocker rig is a bottom fishing set-up where the weight sits right atop the hook and bead on the leader. We send it to the bottom with live pinfish or chunk ballyhoo, and wait for the rod to bend. Another option is the use of a weighted jig head hook with the leader tied straight to the jig head using an advanced clinch knot, uni-knot, or a loop knot. Trolling depends on what you are targeting. For dolphinfish and tuna, it is common to rig ballyhoo on two outrigger rods, while two additional transom rods are outfitted with artificial lures, the live bait sent further out than the others. Diving lures are used for a wide variety of fish. There is a wide assortment of lures available and fish to target. YouTube it.

Also, *YouTube: Carolina rig vs. Knocker rig, Freelining yellowtail,* and *Catching mangrove snapper.* It is possible to catch a mutton snapper with your yellowtail rig, but it is lucky too. When freelining for yellowtail, drop down a bottom rig with a ballyhoo plug. You might even luck into a grouper hiding in structure, but pay close attention, vigilance is key. That grouper has an escape plan already in place. If with a Carolina rig, (weight over swivel, 4' leader, then hook), drop your line down to the bottom, then wind in a few revolutions to avoid getting the weight snagged in the rocks. When the rod bends, the fish has set the hook, you don't need to. But, be quick to raise the tip of the rod straight up, then lower it to your waist as you reel in. You want to reel fast (3 revolutions) as you lower the rod.

Top Spot charts, purchased at any local tackle shop, give lots of good information with regards to spots, waypoints, depths, and hazards to name a few. **MyFWC.com/fishinglines** is a good online resource to FL fishing, as is **Coastal Angler,** and **Salt Water Sportsman** magazines. They clue you in as to what's running where and when – good tips from some of the better local guides. I don't advise purchasing GPS numbers for fishing and lobster spots online. It is the tactic of a con man fishing for suckers. But, you can study a local chart and look for depth changes and coral heads. Otherwise, ask around where you might have some luck, like artificial reefs and patch reefs.

I always keep a respectable distance from other boats. I don't want to invade their chum slick. I definitely don't want to be so close that I can hear their music, or especially – their conversation. That is my rule and advice to you for what is too close. Also, please try not to rock other boats at anchor. I am a big believer in rod holders too. But, when the rod is in a rod holder you still need to pay close attention; nibble, nibble, bend, fish on, and retrieve. If you have multiple rods out, there is little choice but to use rod holders. As for freelining, you are continuously feeding the line out, and feeling the line for a bite. After a minute or two, if no bite, retrieve your bait and start over. If still no bite, reduce your leader size from say, 15 lb to 12 lb.

GEAR

Aside from the rod and reel, the line on the reel spool consists of either monofilament or braid. These are your base lines. It is a preference. I use both in different situations, but I mainly use mono. Braid offers strength but no stretch. But, because it is thinner, more line fits onto the spool. Mono is more angler friendly due to stretch. The fluorocarbon leader, anywhere from 4'+ depending on species, is tied from your mono or braid, either line to line with a Uni, Albright, or via a swivel, and then to your circle hook. Leader is less visible to fish, but not completely invisible. If for instance, the visibility of the water is very clear, here again you might wish to lower your thickness or pound test strength, from say 15 lb to 12 lb. Or, 50 lb to 30 lb.

FISH ON

Rods and reels are designed to do a specific job for a specific purpose. A flexible spinning rod can assist in a good cast. But, that same rod is used in a 4 - step retrieval process once the fish is on. As previously mentioned, don't set the hook. Let the fish set the hook. It is important to remain vigilant, and to retrieve the fish in a fluid if fast motion. The instant that the fish sets the hook, do the following:

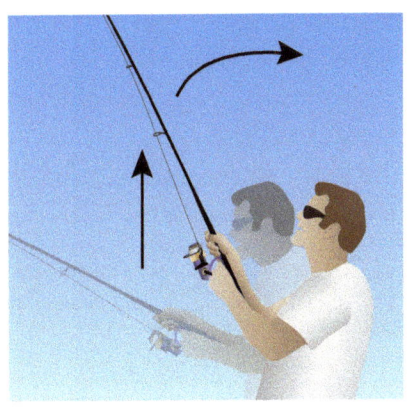

1) Raise the tip end of the rod straight up and close the bail to get the fish off the bottom and away from the rocks.

2) As you lower the rod down to waist height, reel in at a pretty good clip, 3 revolutions. This is repeated a time or two before getting into a regular reel-in motion.

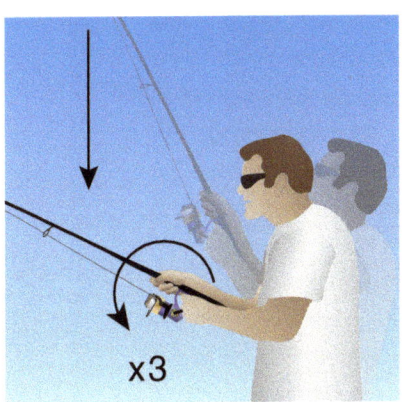

You don't want to over tax your reel gears, so you reel in on the way down. Just be sure to keep the line tight. Your drag is set to where the fish can run some, but you can reel in some too. Don't confuse raising the tip of the rod fast with slamming it into the T-top.

3) Yes, you want to be fast, but you need to be controlled. Bring the fish to the boat, but make sure that you reel in only until the fish reaches the

surface, or approximately 4' away. *Note: Beware of catching the hook on the chum bag and anchor line.*

4) Gently set the butt end of your rod on the deck of the boat so that you can easily reach the leader. Grab the leader and lift it over the gunwale. Or, have a fish safe landing net ready. De-hook the fish, identify it, measure it, and take a photo. Then, either release it, or toss it into the cooler.

In the all too often event that you lost said fish, one of three common scenarios took place: a) You were not paying close enough attention and you got rocked. b) You set the hook, and in doing so, you ripped the hook out of the fishes mouth. c) Or, you were too slow on the retrieve and a predator got your catch. *"Noooo!"* you say? It is one of the more frustrating experiences in fishing – to not know. What was it? The important thing is that you had a fish on. Your rod bent over, and you fought mightily. It's a good thing that you enjoy catch and release. But, to not know what it was – *is just painful.* If the fish are biting you should stay put. When they stop biting for a period of say twenty minutes, or if the fish are consistently small, move on. Control what you can; keep an organized and well stocked tackle box, use the appropriate size line, weight, and hook, and present the bait as natural as possible. Most important perhaps, practice fishing karma and help protect the fishery for others to come. For, what we are all truly targeting is – a memorable experience, and one to save for others to come. So, keep that pretty shell on the sea floor.

Fishing is a bit like golf in that they can both take up several hours of the day. Golf and fishing can get pretty expensive too, and at times, frustrating. There are good holes and bad holes in each sport – times when you experience a hole in one moment and scream with delight, and other times when the hole is less than sweet, and you hope to do better on the next one. Like golf too, there is superstition in fishing. If for example, you catch a nice fish in the first fifteen minutes, be sure NOT to say to yourself, *"Man, I am going to limit out in no time."* Don't do it, don't say it, don't even think it – It is the kiss of death.

Think of fishing as a gift to yourself. But, budget your time too: 3 to 4 hours – like golf. Perhaps early morning or night time fishing suits you better. Work the patch reefs, and move no more than a few times. Or, you might prefer the calm waters of the backcountry instead. No matter where you fish, here or home, structure is key: weeds, trees, rocks, piers, jetties, bridges, and wrecks. Structure, chum, and an assortment of bait generally does the trick. But, don't overdo it, only to get in late when the bugs are biting. You still have to clean up. And, you want to look forward to getting out on the water again. So, rather than limit your post fishing exercise routine to 12 oz curls (beer), you might want to stretch some too. Perhaps you'll even add some legitimate exercise into the mix, like biking and walking prior to your 12 oz curls. It might look like all fun and games, but boating and fishing is a body pounding experience. The more limber the body, the less chance of injury. Live to fish another day. Now, it is well understood that fishing and catching are two separate things, but some guides do actually guarantee a catch or you don't pay. My guarantee is this: when you get a good keeper on the hook, you just got the captain (me) off the hook. And, on a good day, when you say, *"just one more,"* you will likely say it ten more times.

BAIT

Recommended bait here in the Keys includes live pinfish, pilchards, minnows, shrimp, and ballyhoo. If you need to catch pinfish, use the very small #12 hook in your tackle box with tiny bit of squid as bait. You can put an hour aside to catch one pinfish at a time until you have a dozen or more. To trap pinfish, put your trap in 3' - 5' deep turtle grass the day before with a half block of chum. *Note: Use a breaker bar and heavy duty hammer to split the chum block in two. Never use a power saw or sawzall. It will produce a mess, and a timely clean-up.* Then again, most people use a whole block of chum.

© Diane Rome Peebles

Common live bait: Pinfish, Scaled Sardine "Pilchard," Striped Anchovy "Glass Minnow," Shrimp, Ballyhoo

A STARTING POINT

Several local fishing spots in the Lower Keys include **No Name Bridge** MM 30, **Spanish Harbor Bridge** MM 33, **Old 7 Mile Bridge** MM 40, You do need a fishing license to bridge fish from above, or below – go to any local tackle shop, or online. See waypoint coordinates on the **Top Spot** chart. There are coral heads off Big Pine Key. There are artificial reefs worth checking out, e.g., **Big Pine Shoal** at **24° 34.111' N** and **81° 19.541' W** – popular for yellowtail fishing. Ask about bomb holes, patch reefs, and rock piles. Mark similar places where you live. Always have someone on land be aware of your location and expected return time, your float plan.

Here is a fishing package list that I recommend. Start with one rod and a small tackle box (only). If you get hooked on fishing, the following gear is a pretty complete package that will serve you well.

- 2 Penn fast action 7' Spinfisher rods (combo set)
- 2 Penn 4500 Spinfisher spinning reel with 12 lb mono
- 1 Penn 5500 Spinfisher spinning reel with 20 lb mono
- Bubba blade battery operated filet knife
- Tackle box and some plastic containers with dividers
- Top Spot fishing chart (for your area)
- Variety of 1/0 to 7/0 hooks
- Pack of #2, #4, and #6 hooks for pinfish and yellowtail
- 6 each - 1 oz, 1½ oz, and 3 oz egg sinkers
- Pack of very small 80 lb swivels
- Small beads to protect the line from the weight
- 1-2 packs of 7/0 - 9/0 long shank hooks
- Pinfish trap baited with chum and set in turtle grass
- #12 hooks and bits of squid for pinfish and ballyhoo
- Gulp shrimp and mullet artificials (for backcountry)
- 4 bucktail lures, yellow and white
- Fishing pliers, small scissors, and rags
- Small shrimp bucket and aerator, D batteries
- Bait net (for livewell)
- 6' to 8' cast net. I like 3/8". And, 3/16" for smaller bait
- Fish safe (rubber) non-knotted landing net
- A gaff hook
- De-hooker, and a venting and descending tool too
- 24" cooler, 4 - qt or ½ gallon bottles for frozen ice
- Measuring tape (sticker) on your boat
- Gama fluorocarbon leader: 10 lb, 12 lb, 15 lb, 20 lb, 30 lb
- Wire selection: #2 - 18 lb, #3 - 32 lb, and #4 - 44 lb
- An assortment of circle hook jigs: 1/16 oz, 1/8 oz, 1/4 oz
- Knots to learn on YouTube: Uni knot, Advanced clinch knot, loop knot, haywire twist, and *bimini twist*
- Tournament Master chum and a wide mesh chum bag
- Live pinfish, ballyhoo, and shrimp, cutting board
- Plow or Bruce anchor (protects the sea floor better)
- Anchor retrieval kit – buoy, stainless ring set-up

RIGS

Some rigs, or baits, are intended to rest on the bottom for a certain natural presentation, while others are presented as injured but swimming. Here are a few essential rigs.

KNOCKER RIG

A 1 oz - 5 oz+ egg sinker is placed directly above the hook on a 4' leader. For lane snapper, 12 lb+ leader and 1/0 to 2/0 circle hook. For mutton, grouper, etc., 20-30 lb+ leader with 4/0 to 5/0 circle hook. This rig helps to allow the bait to lay inconspicuously and avoid rocking up – compared to a Carolina rig.

CAROLINA RIG

Place an e.g., 2 oz+ egg sinker above an 80 lb swivel and bead. Then tie 4' of 12 lb to 30 lb leader and use a 2/0 to 5/0 circle hook. *Note: This rig can get caught in rocks so pay close attention.* Reel in a few revolutions as precaution. Watch the rod for a nibble, nibble, nibble – and bite / bend.

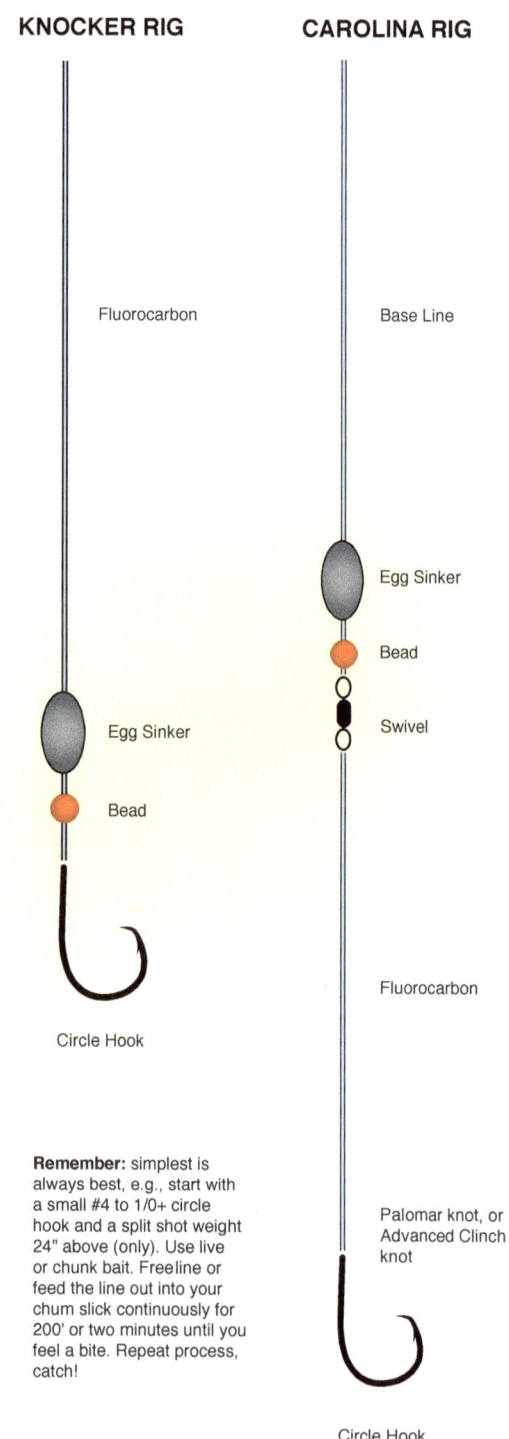

Remember: simplest is always best, e.g., start with a small #4 to 1/0+ circle hook and a split shot weight 24" above (only). Use live or chunk bait. Freeline or feed the line out into your chum slick continuously for 200' or two minutes until you feel a bite. Repeat process, catch!

JIG HEAD RIG

A jig head rig is a very effective low profile weighted hook tied directly to the leader using a loop knot. Add chunk or live bait, to the 1/8 oz+ jig head for a streamlined presentation to freeline, bottom fish, or cast and retrieve, be it with a 12 lb or 20 lb+ leader. The list of targeted species is many: all snapper, seatrout, snook, shark, jacks, mackerel, and then some. As with all rigs, we are imitating the natural behavior of prey in order to entice the predator. This is a great approach, whether with small bait to resemble chum for yellowtail, or larger live bait to resemble larger perhaps distressed prey for snapper, grouper, and cobia. Artificial bait too, is a secret weapon for many. Used in combination with a jig head in shallow freshwater or saltwater environs, **Gulp** and **DOA** artificials get hit after hit, making for a very fun day out fishing and catching.

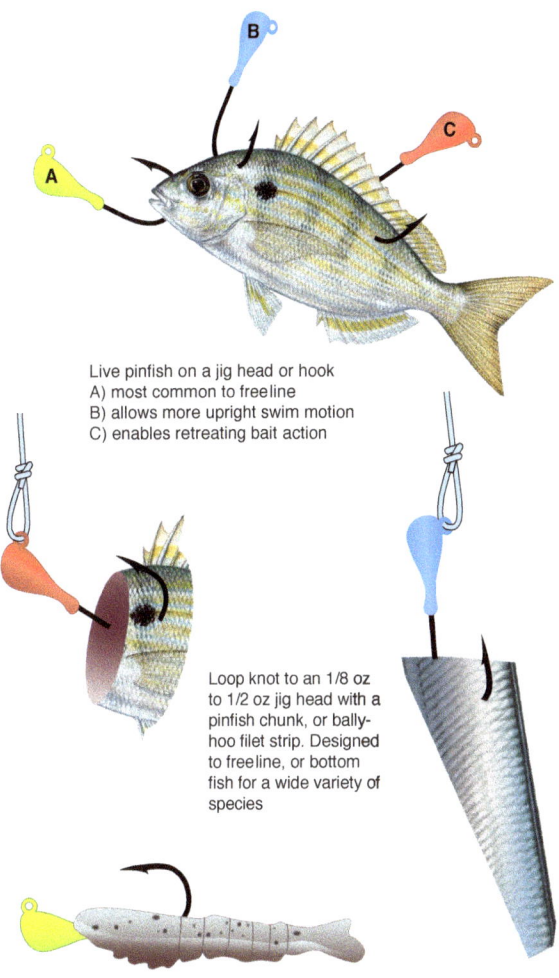

Live pinfish on a jig head or hook
A) most common to freeline
B) allows more upright swim motion
C) enables retreating bait action

Loop knot to an 1/8 oz to 1/2 oz jig head with a pinfish chunk, or ballyhoo filet strip. Designed to freeline, or bottom fish for a wide variety of species

Artificial 3" **Gulp** (penny) shrimp or (pearl) mullet on a jig head, designed to cast, sink, and slow retrieve. Live whole or chunk shrimp on a jig head works great to both freeline and bottom fish.

Loop or Snell knot

Live bait bridle set-up: improves catch odds for mutton snapper, cobia, grouper, tarpon, tuna, and other. Use with 5/0+ circle hook and rubber band or Dacron loop to maximize hook exposure while freelining. If slow trolling, bridle in front of the eyes. Requires a bridle needle, found at tackle shops.

Go to: saltwatersportsman.com/rubber-band-bridle

133

CHICKEN RIG

This is a multi hook rig used for bottom fishing while at anchor, or drift fishing. If for shallow 20' depth, fishing for e.g., lane snapper, use only 15 lb leader and a 2 oz bank sinker. Tie a series of surgeon knots for each of the three hooks and sinker. Do this by doubling the line into a loop and tying an overhand knot, then passing it through the loop twice. Another option is to use 3-way swivels instead of tying knots.

A heavier duty chicken rig is also known as an up down rig, or a deep drop rig. In this case, use 30 lb+ leader with just one or two 5/0+ hooks above the weight 18" apart. The 8 oz+ bank sinker is mainly dependent upon the depth and current. You might use 65 lb braid, and 40 lb leader, and perhaps a 12 oz sinker. The concept remains the same.

YouTube: Surgeon Knot and Chicken Rig.

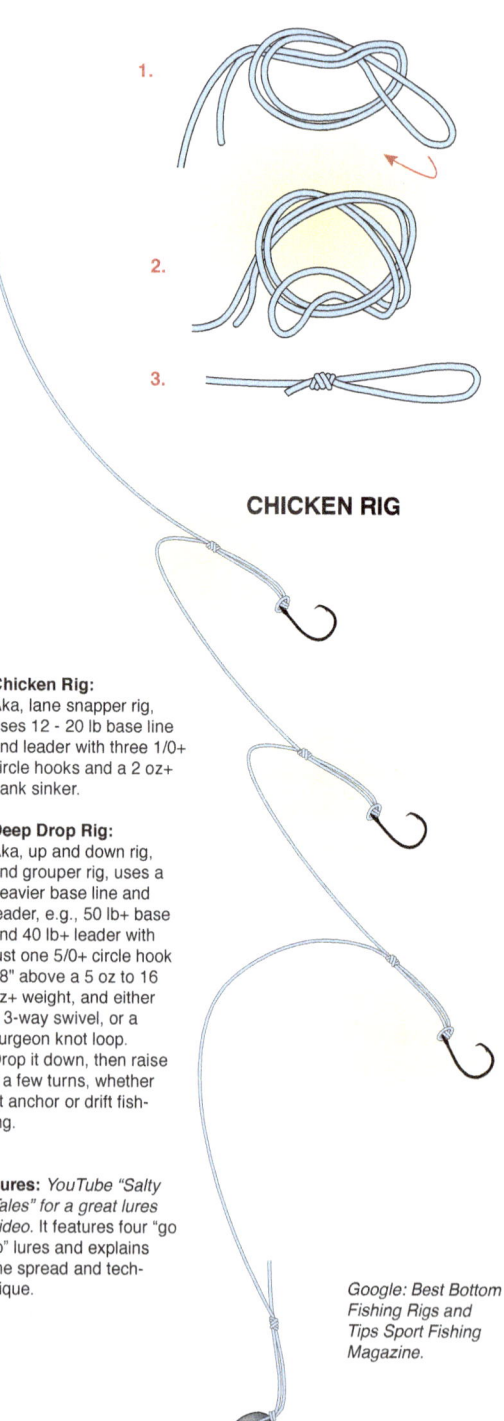

Chicken Rig:
Aka, lane snapper rig, uses 12 - 20 lb base line and leader with three 1/0+ circle hooks and a 2 oz+ bank sinker.

Deep Drop Rig:
Aka, up and down rig, and grouper rig, uses a heavier base line and leader, e.g., 50 lb+ base and 40 lb+ leader with just one 5/0+ circle hook 18" above a 5 oz to 16 oz+ weight, and either a 3-way swivel, or a surgeon knot loop. Drop it down, then raise it a few turns, whether at anchor or drift fishing.

Lures: *YouTube "Salty Tales" for a great lures video*. It features four "go to" lures and explains the spread and technique.

Google: Best Bottom Fishing Rigs and Tips Sport Fishing Magazine.

BASIC BOTTOM RIG

Base Line
20 lb - 80 lb
Braid or Mono
20 lb with Bimini twist

3-Way Swivel
(This can also be two single swivels, one for the sliding weight, used with a quick release snap swivel)

12"+ of 15 lb mono

24 oz Bank Sinker

30 feet (+ or –)
30 lb (+ or –)
Mono

For particular searches such as... How to butterfly ballyhoo, How to target mutton snapper, How to target cobia, How to target grouper, How to target blackfin tuna, etc., Google your "How to" query, followed by "saltwater sportsman" for some very thorough information. You will learn a lot!

You should also visit georgepoveromo.com for tons of other great information. George Poveromo is hands-down, the ultimate mentor's mentor.

80 lb + swivel

4 feet
30 lb+ fluoro

2/0 - 7/0+ circle hook

BASIC BOTTOM RIG

For depths 50' to 200'+. Tie the base line to a 3-way swivel. Then, tie a long e.g., 20' - 30' leader of 50 lb monofilament with an 80 lb swivel at the end. This is where you place 4' to 6'+ of 30 lb fluorocarbon leader. If for mutton snapper, cobia, or grouper, use a 5/0 to 7/0 circle hook with live or chunk bait. On the third eye of the 3-way swivel, attach 2' to 4' of 12 lb fluoro for the 8 oz+ bank sinker onto a surgeon loop, (lighter test strength.) In the event that you get rocked, the 12 lb line will break, whereas much stronger test will not. This rig can be modified, lighter or stronger, based on targeted species, depth, and current. For example, it could be 80 lb braid and 60 lb leader, or 50 lb braid to a 40 lb leader. Drop it down, lift the weight off the bottom 3 to 6 turns, and drift with live or chunk bait.

Google: Basic Rigs with Bouncer Smith / YouTube

BACKCOUNTRY FISHING

On the Gulf side waters of the FL Keys, several miles north of US 1, is an area known as the backcountry. It is what the Keys are famous for – natural splendor. The backcountry presents a learning curve, both fishing wise and navigation wise. But, with some local knowledge as explained here, you might have some good luck.

Fishing in general is migratory dependent. Fish come and go due to feeding habits, water temperature, and spawning needs. The Keys are famous too, for the large variety species that can be caught on a given day. The backcountry is a big territory with a lot of fish stories to tell: bonefish, tarpon, permit, cobia, lobster, grouper, snapper, seatrout, mackerel, barracuda, and shark to name a few. The mangrove islands, seagrass beds, algae life, and a large variety of sponges present a shallow water ecosystem like no other.

Flats fishing is a specialized field. It is poling in soul filled solitude through shallow water wilderness in search of something sacred. But, all is not flats fishing in the backcountry. Light tackle anglers exist, though relatively few. The seasoned angler knows to keep distance from the flats guide and client during their bucket list quest in fishing mecca. There is an understanding here – or should be.

Resident snapper find relief and food year round in seagrass beds, bomb holes, and of course, mangrove islands, their original nursery.

Bomb holes are numerous spots mostly on the bay side where during WWII military exercises were ongoing, and planes would drop practice munitions leaving behind both light colored ledges, and dark deep holes. Bomb holes are scattered throughout, but you need to find them. As for ledges, look for light spots in grass channels.

In warmer months, the Gulf waters, aka the backcountry bathtub can exceed 90° water temperature. It is a time where one might not see another boat for hours, or all day. Permit, resident bonefish and tarpon can still be found, and caught. The flats guides earn their pay, plied from many years of trial and error – all for the client's reward.

Come May, migrating tarpon arrive. In summer, fish spawn, and on a particular full moon in May or June, palolo worms hatch. Then, lobster season opens. Such is the cycle of life in the Florida Keys. Before you know it, cooler months come. Larger mangrove snapper return to the grass flats. Then, cobia, mackerel, and seatrout arrive, as do folks from cooler climates – many to fish.

Backcountry fishing is more relaxing compared to ocean side fishing. A couple of backcountry guides that come to mind include; **Captain Aaron Snell** *305-304-0261 (flats fishing)*, **Captain Will Benson** *305-923-6114 (flats fishing)*, and **Captain Larry White** *(recreational, navigation, eco, and fishing) 305-393-4153*. One can cast artificials in the grass beds for snapper, jacks, and seatrout. Or, freeline shrimp into a chum slick for mackerel. Others jig with chunk or live bait. You might prefer to troll a ballyhoo or tube lure for mackerel and barracuda, or cast a spoon, drop a jig head, or use surface popper.

If you come upon a wreck, you might drift or anchor and freeline a live pinfish in hopes of landing a cobia. If you are in grass, and catching small mangrove snapper, try to cast back further. The small fish generally gather near the chum, while the larger fish stay back. It is here too, where you might luck into a grouper. Out further in the Gulf, wrecks and rock pile spots are worth a go. See the area Top Spot chart. Whether fly fishing, bottom fishing, freelining, casting and retrieving, or trolling – the backcountry is a magical place.

BRIDGE FISHING

When bridge fishing, whether atop the bridge or in a boat beneath it, it is important to first look at the tide chart. It also helps to check the tide where you fish – the day before if possible. You might have noticed that the tide chart and the actual turn of the tide is off by perhaps an hour or two. How can this be?

There is a phenomena known as tidal coefficient which changes from day to day based on the moon, sun, and earth rotation. A coefficient rate of 50 is an average to calm coefficient. It means that there will not be a big current under the bridge, and that the predicted tides will be closer to the chart. *Note: Most of North America has tides every 6 hours, or four tides every twenty-four hour period.*

A high coefficient of say 96+, means that there is a lot of water flow from one tide to the other, and that there will be a strong current. This strong current also translates into delayed tide direction. You might find, with a strong tidal coefficient, that a predicted tide of noon might not happen until 2PM. If it is coupled with a strong tail wind, the delay is even greater. The most obvious water flow in the Keys, and where you live, happens at bridges. This is the a place where water flows from wide to narrow, and then wide again – from one side to the other. The final hour of the tide, whether at low or high tide, is generally strongest with a grand finale effect of sorts. You just don't want to get to a bridge, or anywhere, at slack tide.

You will need to select a tide where it is low and rising or high and falling, in that you want current. Some say low to rising is better. Bridges are also viewed as structure. And, fish know that the tidal flow at bridges delivers a meal to them at every tide like clockwork. You want to position your boat so that you are on the side of the bridge that is flowing from, not flowing to. So, if tide is moving from north to south, you want to anchor on the north side of the bridge. Check the contour lines too – fish are also attracted to depth change.

Your anchor is set. Your motor is off. Your kill switch shim is disengaged. Your chum is out. You get organized. Your rods have 20 lb mono, a 2 oz to 5 oz egg sinker, Bimini twist, and a 12 lb leader. It's good to have at least two rods in case one malfunctions or breaks.

Your fluorocarbon leader is 4' in length. All you have from here is a 2/0 to 4/0 hook – also with an advanced clinch knot. You have a variety of bait: ballyhoo chunks, live pinfish, pilchards, and shrimp. Your weight is based on the current flow: light current 1 oz, stronger current, 2 oz to 5 oz. You are here to relax, but you also want to see your rod bend. The chum generally takes ten to fifteen minutes. The bite might be on or off. It could get better in fifteen minutes or not at all. So, after a half hours time, if no action, you move to another spot. Another approach to bridge fishing is drift fishing along the pilings. The idea being, to pull the fish from piling to piling and increase your odds. If a light current use chum. If strong – no chum.

Note: If you are fishing from an actual bridge and not in a boat, it helps to have a long line for your chum bag. And, another long line for your catch net. Of course, you will also have drinks for yourself, and another cooler and ice for your catch. You might even bring shade. Some bridge anglers have very elaborate set-ups: coolers on wheels, carts, multiple rods, rod holders, and perhaps, chairs. In any case, have your fishing license with you. Don't be surprised if the game warden comes for a visit. Don't get caught with under sized, or over the limit. Ignorance is not bliss. If you prefer a bridge fishing guide, who supplies all of the gear, contact Ryan at **Land-Boat Charters** *305-204-9772* and *fishthebridges.com*. Like most inshore fishing, bridges often produce best results in cooler months.

IN CONCLUSION

If I had known ten years ago what I know today, I would have done things differently. And, as a result, I would have saved a ton of time and money. It is true for you too. You don't have to buy the entire tackle shop. It will not make you a better angler. It is in fact, more likely to slow down your learning curve. Thank goodness for pegboards as a way to organize said purchases. It was not until I bought my first pegboard that I realized that I had way too much stuff – the store.

The only way to become a better angler, like anything, is to put the time in. This doesn't mean that you have to do it all: troll, vertical jig, bottom fish, freeline, deep drop, and fly fish. You don't need to flats, reef, and wreck fish. Or, to buy kites for sailfish, and heavy duty rods and lights for swordfish. Just find what you enjoy and be you. Speaking of which, I have friends who solely fish for porgy.

Remember, there are many different ways to target, tie, present, bait, and catch fish. Find the way that works best for you. Ballyhoo pin rig with a spring? – Great! Bare treble hook on wire with a live pilchard and little drag? Hello kingfish! Cedar plug and feather lures in 150' - 200' near sunset? It's tuna time! 20' long 40 lb leader in 170' with a live pinfish and a 12 oz weight above the swivel for mutton? Hold on! The point is, there is no one right way, except when what you consistently do; target, tie, present, and bait – catches fish.

The easiest way to start out in my opinion is: 1) Fishing for mangrove snapper over a grassy channel in 10' of water on the bay side of the Keys. Freeline out live shrimp, and / or live pinfish for bigger snapper. Then, 2) Learn how to catch yellowtail on the reef. *See yellowtail page 146.* 3) While yellowtailing, send down a ballyhoo plug on a long leader and 3 oz weight to perhaps entice a mutton snapper. 4) Try slow trolling for grouper with a 20'+ yellowtail looking Rapala or Nomad diving lure in Hawk Channel along the dropoff and rise edges, and over patch reef areas just inside the reef. And, 5) Last but not least, troll with ballyhoo during summer months in 300' to 650'+ deep water for mahi, and out back in 10' - 20' for mackerel. These techniques are certain to fulfill most all fishing desires. Or, just fish for porgy in 40' deep water. Even the bridges are on fire some months, with snapper and yellow jacks in Winter, and tarpon, come April, May.

Fortunately, our offshore or 600' to 800'+ deep water here in the Keys only takes a half hour to 45 minutes to get out to, rather than several hours in the case of many places to the west and north. That said, when you do go offshore pick your weather and conditions responsibly. Have an Epirb on your person, not buried somewhere. Bring food and water. Make sure that your fuel is full. Wear a lifejacket. And, let someone on land know where you are, and what time you expect to return. *Note: All boaters should know how to close their livewell seacock while blindfold, and with the bilge half full of water too. The open livewell seacock is the most common culprit of boats that sink.*

I am not that person who says, *"That's why they call it fishing and not catching."* In fact, if not for catching I might be lured by pickleball instead. I need to catch, so I put in the time one species at a time. I watch the tides, and have multiple baits - including live bait whenever possible.

Remember, fish swim. That is to say, fish migrate, and the season for many species is often limited to a few months. My friend, Joe asked me if I knew of the three T's? I said no. He said *"Tide, temperature, and time."* I asked him if he knew of the three D's. He said no. I said, *"Debris, de-birds, and de-weeds."* Know your T's & D's.

Night fishing is a whole other learning curve, but most of the time, very productive. Get out to the reef in 60' - 80' over structure an hour before sunset so to get properly set up. Use a head lamp at dark, and otherwise lights out. Get a strong 1600 lumen or greater spotlight rigged to your T-top, and know how to dim your GPS backlight for your midnight or later return. It can otherwise be blinding.

Summer deep drop fishing on calm days can be especially productive when targeting Blueline Tilefish, Queen Snapper, and 40+ lb Snowy Grouper. Deep drop season is limited to two months, July and August. But, to get back to a point I made earlier: with so much variety in fishing, it is easy to go overboard on your tackle purchases. You can easily become hooked, but try to control your spending. For me, trolling can be boring. I have to find birds, debris, or a weed line before I start to troll. Otherwise, I go back in and reef fish. But, when I do find birds, and trolling is productive, I love it!

There are not enough mentors out there other than YouTube. And, perhaps your dad. Only buy what you need to start. That is my message to you in these pages. Of course, you will need a filet knife, pliers, scissors, and a de-hooker, all must-haves, but otherwise start slow. Get your fishing license, purchase a rod / reel combo set-up, 15 lb braided line, or maybe just mono to start. Mono is more angler friendly due to its stretch. Get various size leader lines, hooks, weights, and start with live shrimp as bait, or better yet, start with frozen yet thawed shrimp, so as to not need a bucket and aerator – yet. Use frozen squid too, and ballyhoo chunks.

For trolling, all you need is a pack of mono rigged ballyhoo. If you wish to put a skirt over it, buy a small variety, no more than six total. And, don't clutter your tackle box with said skirts. Rig them the evening before or morning of, then put them on top of a bag of ice in a cooler. The bait that you don't use can be used the next day, or tossed. So, only prepare 6 to 10 for the outing, half of them as weedless. *Google: Poveromo weedless ballyhoo rig.* Over the years I have accumulated dozens of skirts and lures, half of which are now retired as art decor for my screened-in room pegboard. It is the same with artificial lures, limit that purchase to six total. If you do this, I just saved you hundreds, and possibly thousands of dollars. So, this book has already paid for itself 100 fold.

Continue this discipline with weights, hooks, jig heads, leader, poppers, and everything else. You don't need to fill an entire pegboard, just a relatively small tackle box with the right stuff: one pack each of 1/0 - 5/0 circle hooks, one 25 pack of 1/16 oz, and 1/4 oz weighted circle hooks to start. A small variety of egg sinkers from split shots to 3 oz, if only a few of each. One spool of each, 12 lb, 15 lb, and 20 lb, fluorocarbon leader to start. If you discover that you do in fact prefer the fishing pole to pickleball, streamline your start; mangrove snapper, yellowtail, porgy, troll with diving lures and ballyhoo for mahi. Watch more YouTube videos. In short, put the time in to see what you like best.

If you eventually get into deep drop fishing, secure your 4 lb to 6 lb lead weight with a 12" or so loop of 30 lb mono using a uni to uni knot to the top of the weight rather than connecting the weight directly to a 150 lb snap swivel. Worse case scenario, you will only lose the lead, and not hundreds of feet of line too. Also, remember to create a deep drop check list before you go out to 600+ feet of water. You don't want to go all that way and realize that you forgot e.g., your power cable at home.

As your fishing fever expands, so too can your purchases, but do so responsibly. In that case, you might need a 5500 combo set-up, and perhaps a 7500 rod and reel set-up, a cast net, pinfish bait trap, holding pen, a crimper, crimps, snap swivels, and so on. If such is the case, you are most definitely hooked. Say goodbye to thousands of dollars. Now is the time to get an airline credit card so that your purchases can at least go toward flight points. And, find yourself a fishing buddy, one who can help share the expenses, if only bait, chum, fuel contribution, and clean-up. As you practice more, and ask more seasoned anglers advice, you can then make more investment. My porgy fishing friends make sure to keep costs low. They catch shrimp at night for bait, sometimes 1000+, and fish for porgy every fair weather day using a Carolina rig with 1 oz - 3 oz sliding sinker in 40' deep water on the ocean side, or near a contour drop off in the 30' depth range.

GOOD LUCK

No two words are more frequently associated with fishing than good luck. And, for good reason. You are either sure to relax, or get completely frustrated – that is the game. The main thing is to go easy on yourself. If you can hire a guide to help you find a few reliable spots, you should. If you secure the right guide as mentor, it can save years of frustration. It is a luxury for sure, but If you can afford it the learning curve is swift compared to going it alone. If not, perhaps you could split the cost of the charter with another person.

If you still can't afford it, I completely understand. Start with bridge fishing, with a coefficient in the 75 range. Go to **Tides4Fishing.com** for this information. Know water temperature, wind conditions, incoming or outgoing tide, and weather. Have a drag indicator of some sort in place – a lobster buoy, MOB mark, or another boat to monitor your position.

I can recommend the following Lower Keys tackle shops: **The Tackle Box**, Marathon, **Lower Keys Tackle**, Big Pine Key, **Jigs Bait and Tackle**, Big Pine Key, **Cudjoe Sales**, Cudjoe Key, **Key West Marine Hardware,** in Key West, **West Marine**, Marathon and Key West, and **Key West Bait & Tackle,** *if only for a beer.*

The following pages might be the sole reason that you purchased this book in the first place. **Tips & Targeting** and the **Q&A.** I hope it saves you money and helps you catch. Tight lines and happy fishing!

TIPS & TARGETING WITH CAPTAIN JIMMY GAGLIARDINI

YELLOWTAIL SNAPPER

© Diane Rome Peebles

SIZE: Less than a foot in coastal shallows and 1-3 lbs on deep reefs. Larger yellowtail, "flags" up to 4 or 5 lbs is not uncommon. Some run to 7 or 8 lbs and 24"+ in length.

HABITAT: Best fishing depths in most areas are 60' to 100', with nearly all the "flags" generally coming from the deeper habitat.

MIN LENGTH: 12 inches

EDIBILITY: Excellent

LIMIT: 10 per day (10 snapper aggregate limit)

TACKLE: 7' lightweight spinning rod with Penn Spinfisher VII 4500 reel, or similar. Start with 15 lb line and a 10 lb leader, and a very small but strong #4 hook. If a good current, use a weighted jig head. The goal is to mimic the chum and oats drift and sink action.

BAIT: Chum liberally, add cups of oats mix with each drift. Small dead baits—cut fish, bonito, shrimp, glass minnows, similar in size and buoyancy to chum. A good current, good chum slick, and a streamlined presentation of line and bait is key to catching yellowtail.

FISHING TECHNIQUE: Open bail, freeline. Continuously feed out for up to 100 feet or 2 minutes. Feel for bite, then reel in. If no bite, repeat the process. Early morning / sun-up is the best time to catch.

OUTING & TACTIC

Captain Jimmy Gagliardini and I went out in search of yellowtail snapper. We would keep nothing less than a 15", even though 12" is the legal minimum. Our actual goal was 20"+, aka "flag." Captain Jimmy uses a technique of prepping a 7 lb chum block in a 5 gallon bucket, with 2 gallons of seawater to thaw. He then adds about 5 pounds of dry oats to fill a 5 gallon bucket mix.

When yellowtail fishing – chum. That is the do or die rule. And, you want to do what commercial yellowtail fishermen and women do, chum liberally. That said, commercial yellowtail people use as much as 200+ lbs of chum and a 50 lb bag of oats per 5 hour outing. You will likely use one 7 lb bock per hour and perhaps 5 lbs of oats. We were in 90' of water. Prior to dropping the anchor, Jimmy watched his drift on the chart plotter so to position where the chum and oats will be most effective. It takes about 15 to 30 minutes to see a good school gathered behind the boat. But, much less time when it's a regular spot. 65' to 90' is generally good for larger yellowtail.

As with most species, the big fish lurk further back. Our intention was not to limit out per se, but to catch dinner. If no bite in 30 minutes, we move. If two anglers, it helps to have two chum slicks going when yellowtailing. Also, have a 5 gallon bucket for your chum bag(s) when taken out of the water to move. Otherwise, it is a mess! Start with light gauge 10 lb line and leader, and a small but strong #4 hook. Keep the bail open and feed the line back, as if not attached to a line. Find your inner bait. If cut off regularly, up your leader to 12 lb. Chum is key – current too. The oats mix helps bring the fish to the surface. Adding handfuls of minnows and pilchards to the mix can result in a feeding frenzy, and bigger fish. You can't have too much bait.

Catching a 12" yellowtail is fun but a 20"+ flag is a thrill. One "flag" is plenty for a meal or two. Yellowtail are leery. They combine surface feeding with bottom fleeing. Handle all fish with care – wet hands, and never a towel. The slime on the fish is its protection. It is important too, to support their weight horizontally as you de-hook. And, remember, you don't have to limit out. Take only what you think you will eat. *Note: When snapper fishing, use circle hooks.*

TIPS & TARGETING WITH CAPTAIN JIMMY GAGLIARDINI

BLACK GROUPER

© Diane Rome Peebles

SIZE: Up to 48 inches, more common is 24" to 30" and 15 to 25 lbs. Of course, the most common catch is one inch below the legal limit.

HABITAT: Coastal waters near structure such as reefs, mangroves and seagrass. Larger black grouper can be found near wrecks and artificial reefs in 50' to 200' water. But, also in shallow ledges.

MIN LENGTH: 24 inches   **EDIBILITY:** Excellent

LIMIT: Atlantic: 1 per day / Gulf of Mexico Federal Waters: 4 per day

TACKLE: Grouper fishing from a boat typically involves live bait fished on the bottom with a Carolina rig, e.g., 2 oz+ egg sinker, swivel, 6' leader and 5/0 circle hook. Or, a dbl hook chicken rig: 2 oz+ weight on 30 lb leader bottom, and 5/0+ hooks on surgeon loop 18" above.

BAIT: Live grunt, pinfish, live or chunk ballyhoo, and trolling diving lures. You can also try a weighted jig head, or a Knocker rig.

FISHING TECHNIQUE: Vigilance is key. Put the beer down. Keep an eye on the rod tip. That, or get rocked – repeatedly. The grouper already has an escape plan in mind. Keep a tight drag. Once on, raise the rod, and reel in on the way down. *For vertical bait presentation, Google: Chicken rig for snapper and grouper / YouTube.*

OUTING & TACTIC

Black grouper is always a prized fish. Red grouper and gag grouper is a good second. There is, in fact, a pretty large variety of grouper. Another prized grouper, found in deep water, e.g., 600' to 800'+ is snowy grouper – most often caught by deep dropping, or using an electric powered reel. Mutton snapper can caught similarly, but different. *Google: Basic bottom rig with Bouncer Smith / YouTube.*

As fish in shallow water become more scarce, some anglers "deep drop," using electric reels in deeper waters, 500' to 1000'+ deep. Fishing is not what it was twenty years ago. And, now with climate change and water temperature rise, it is not getting any easier. Electric reels can deliver your catch to the surface in minutes. But, it is a technology that should be limited in its use so not to overfish.

Some hard core anglers still fish in a traditional style of rod and reel, and crank that monster up from the bottom, even from 500'+. This amazing effort translates into as many as 400 rotations on a spinning reel, and 200 rotations on a high ratio conventional reel, not including the back and forth fight. And, that is with no less than 12 oz to 32 oz of weight added on – just to get the line to the bottom. This approach is still sport, and a well deserved catch.

Black grouper are most often found in rocks, so anglers commonly experience multiple cut-offs in the process. It can be frustrating. Remember the black grouper escape plan – they secretly get your bait to the rocks before you even know that you have a fish on. But, there are other times too, when your rod bends in the rod holder and you react in time to get that beauty to the surface. You can also sometimes wait out a rocked grouper, as if you cut the line but didn't – and catch. If you're lucky, it's a keeper. In truth, if you're lucky, you just get to see what it was, because all too often – you don't. Seek out shallower humps surrounded by deeper water, e.g., 18' surrounded by 24', then drop a pinfish down on a Carolina rig. On the Gulf side waters, grouper are often sought by anglers in ledges / white spots in grass. Otherwise; hope to catch one while fishing for mangrove snapper over a patch reef. Or, try targeting grouper with diving lures in 25' to 45' depth along the patch reefs.

TIPS & TARGETING WITH CAPTAIN JIMMY GAGLIARDINI

MANGROVE / GRAY SNAPPER

© Diane Rome Peebles

SIZE: Common 13 to 24 inches

HABITAT: Coastal waters near structure throughout reef and patch reef year round. On the Gulf side, in the backcountry grass beds in Winter months, the bigger mangrove snapper tend to be further back from the chum – where little ones gather. So, cast back.

MIN LENGTH: 10" / Federal waters 12"   **EDIBILITY:** Excellent

LIMIT: 5 per day / Federal waters 3 miles+ out 10 per day

TACKLE: 7' lightweight spinning rod with Penn Spinfisher VII 4500 reel, or similar. 12 lb mono line to 12 lb leader. Bimini twist or spider hitch to leader and jig head. Or, use a 1 oz+ egg sinker on your leader, directly atop a 2/0+ circle hook = Knocker rig.

BAIT: Ballyhoo chunks, pinfish chunks, live pinfish, and big shrimp. Start with one block of chum.

FISHING TECHNIQUE: Anchor in 30' on the perimeter of a patch reef and chum back to it. Drop down a Carolina rig toward the patch. On the Gulf side, fish the perimeter of ledges, 6'+ white spots in the grass channels. Freeline chunk bait on a 2/0 hook and split shot 24" above. A low profile 1/8 oz weighted circle hook works great.

OUTING & TACTIC

Captain Jimmy and I went out in search of mangrove snapper – a perennial favorite as table fare, and very fun to catch. Mangrove snapper, aka Gray snapper, are most often found in patch reefs. Patch reefs are isolated outcroppings of coral that are in close proximity to each other but are physically separated by sand.

If you can, head out to the reef when the water is particularly blue and search out patch reefs as reconnaissance. In 25' to 45' depth you will see many patches or dark spots that clearly stand out from the sandy bottom around it. Study your sonar too. This combined information can supply you with patch reefs and structure to mark – and test. If it proves a winner, keep it as one of your GPS numbers.

Upon your arrival, determine the drift. Then, anchor just up current of the patch reef in sand. Put your chum bag out so it flows over the patch. Drop your bait to the bottom and reel in two revolutions to lift your weight. Your bait might be ballyhoo chunks, cut pinfish, live pinfish, or pilchard. Shrimp are good too, especially in wintertime when shrimp are big. Place one on a jig head, and see how soon the nibble starts. But, wait for the rod to bend.

Start with a Carolina rig: 20 lb base line with a Bimini twist (making it 40 lb), with a 1 oz+ weight above the swivel. Then, your 12 lb 4' leader to a 2/0+ circle hook. You also have the option of a Knocker rig, that lays on the bottom. Or, a small jig head / circle hook. Set the drag to a balanced, fish pull / reel in ratio, aka pretty tight. Whatever your rig, the rule for fishing in the Keys is to let the fish set the hook, not you. Nibble, nibble, bend (hook set). Lift the rod so it is almost pointing straight up. Close the bail. Lower the rod to waist level and reel in 3 revolutions on the down motion. Put the butt end of the rod against your hip for max leverage. Bring the fish to the surface, 3' from the tip of the rod. Grab the center of the rod with your non reeling hand. Raise the tip, grab the leader, and stand your rod up. The fish is now where you can dehook it. Open the bail for more freedom. Ten inches is keeper size, but you might wish to keep only fish 14" and larger. You might also keep just five fish between the two of you rather than the ten fish limit for two anglers, or only what you need.

TIPS & TARGETING WITH CAPTAIN JIMMY GAGLIARDINI

MUTTON SNAPPER

© Diane Rome Peebles

SIZE: Up to 30 inches

HABITAT: Coastal waters near structure. Commonly found over sand, at the reef. And, in deeper 100' - 200' depth around wrecks.

MIN LENGTH: 18 inches

EDIBILITY: Excellent

LIMIT: 5 per day (10 snapper aggregate limit)

TACKLE: 5500 spinning set-up, or conventional if deeper for faster retrieval. 20 lb mono base with a Bimini twist, 2 oz to 8 oz+ egg sinker depending on depth and current, and a 25' length of 30 lb leader with a 5/0 hook. As with all fish and knots, etc, *YouTube: Catching Mutton, Best fishing knots, and Chicken rigs.*

BAIT: Live pinfish, live pilchards, live or cut ballyhoo, big live shrimp. *A 10 lb leader and #12 hook with a bit of squid can catch live ballyhoo.*

FISHING TECHNIQUE: Anchor at the drop off of the reef in 75' - 90' or drift fish from 75' to 200'. You can vertical jig or use live pinfish. The perimeter of wrecks is another common mutton target. You can use two swivels, one for the weight to slide, and the other for the leader. Or, use a 3-way swivel. Mutton are leery of weight. The more bottom current, the longer the leader. *YouTube: Descending device.*

OUTING & TACTIC

Nowadays, mutton snapper are harder to target than to happen upon while fishing for yellowtail, mangrove snapper, and grouper. That is, unless one is: a) spearfishing with scuba gear, or b) west of Key West in prime grouper and mutton snapper territory.

If one were to target mutton snapper, there are a couple of approaches. One way is to find a wreck in 100'+ deep water, figure out your drift direction, then a) drifting a long leader down and crank the weight up a few turns, or b) just off the reef in a sandy bottom. Anchor and drop down a live pinfish, big shrimp, or pilchard on a jig head. *Note: No chum is required while deep water drift fishing.*

The weight varies depending on depth and current. If 200' you might use a 5 oz to 12 oz+ sliding weight before the leader. Best to place a swivel on the line to slide, then another swivel tied to the eye of your main line. Your 30' leader of 30 lb fluorocarbon, tied to the swivel, also acts to prevent the weight from sliding toward your 5/0 circle hook. Crank your weight up 5 or 6 turns to get it a good 10' off of the bottom. *Google: Basic Bottom Rig with Bouncer Smith*, and also *GeorgePoveromo.com* for some really great tips on saltwater rigs.

Mutton snapper are: a) smart, and b) weight leery. So, in this case, we suspend a weight way back on a sliding swivel using 24" of 15 lb mono. We use lighter gauge mono for the bank weight, so it can break off if snagged. You only reel in until the swivel weight reaches the tip of the rod. Hand line in the remaining 30' leader. After a good fight, the mutton get pretty worn out. Just make sure it is legal.

If fishing over the reef, or on the perimeter of a patch reef, anchor and use chum to lure the mutton to you. The key to mutton fishing is generally achieved by using a long leader. But, if e.g., yellowtail fishing or in 60' to 100' depth try your luck with light tackle, 20 lb base, Bimini twist, and a 20 lb+ leader to a jig head and live pinfish. You might also try a ballyhoo plug, and see which they prefer on the day. Mutton snapper is one of those catches that brings great satisfaction to your fishing day, and if a keeper, a nice reward too. In short, similar to grouper, there is no one way to catch mutton snapper.

TIPS & TARGETING WITH CAPTAIN JIMMY GAGLIARDINI

SPOTTED SEATROUT / SPECKLED TROUT

© Diane Rome Peebles

SIZE: Up to 39 inches, common to 14 inches

HABITAT: Coastal waters over sand bottoms or seagrass beds.

MIN LENGTH: slot size 15" to 19", except one allowed over 19"

LIMIT: 3 per licensed angler per day. Always check Fish Rules app

EDIBILITY: Very Good

TACKLE: A lightweight spinning set up with 10 lb to 12 lb mono and a similar leader. Try a 1/0 circle hook with a split shot 24" above.

BAIT: Gulp shrimp or mullet (artificial) on a lightweight jig head. Also, slow retrieve live shrimp, or chunk bait on a small 1/0 circle hook.

FISHING TECHNIQUE: Anchor in 6' to 8' deep seagrass. Minimal presentation, 1/0 circle hook and 1/4 oz split shot 24" above, with chunk ballyhoo or pinfish. Freeline continuously. Or, if no current, let sit. If using artificial, reel in slowly with a slight occasional jerk.

SUSTAINABLE FISHING: Please handle all fish carefully — with wet hands, and hold horizontally, before a quick release to the water.

OUTING & TACTIC

Speckled trout is a fun fish to catch, and a good fish to start out fishing. They are relatively easy to catch. Trout prefer water temperatures of 65 to 77, so winter months are the best time to catch.

You will find speckled trout in relatively shallow water: in channels, over grass, and under weed lines too. You can either drift fish, or anchor while using shrimp and mullet type artificials on a jig head. We generally fish speckled trout on the Gulf side in the backcountry, but they can be caught in the shallows on the ocean side too.

Seatrout fishing can be a gift when mangrove snapper fishing is slow, especially to the charter guide. Both fish can be targeted the same, whether using chunk bait or artificials. If artificial, allow the jig head to sink to the bottom, then retrieve at a very slow pace, while jerking the lure on occasion. You are mimicking an injured shrimp. You can also surface fish speckled trout using a surface plug.

You want to be in an area where mullet are, and in relatively shallow depths, 4' to 8' of water. There are some great videos on YouTube. Mullet mud up the bottom when feeding and can often help to locate seatrout. Anchor and slow retrieve, or drift fish. An outgoing tide over grassbeds, and along side channels, is another good place to start.

It is recommended to wet your hands while handling seatrout (and all fish), so not to wipe off their protective slime coating. Please get in the habit of using a de-hooker, and try not to touch the fish whenever possible. Or, de-hook in the water. If gut swallowed, cut the line.

Also, a non-knotted net, or rubber net, is safer for fish intended to release. I use a rubber fishmonger apron cut at the waist, so to protect the slime coating of fish, and to save fishing shirts from blood stains.

The ideal fishing outfit for seatrout is with 10 lb test line and a 10 lb to 12 lb+ leader on a light weight rod. The fly rod set-up should be a 7 wt. with 20 lb backing and a 12 lb leader. The tan and white minnow combination works great.

TIPS & TARGETING WITH CAPTAIN JIMMY GAGLIARDINI

DOLPHINFISH / MAHI

© Diane Rome Peebles

SIZE: Up to 63 inches, common 24", can be 15 - 25 lbs+ and larger.

HABITAT: Offshore 10 to 30 miles. Gulf Stream, 200' - 650'+ depth. Attracted to sargassum weed lines, debris, and color change.

MIN LENGTH: Atlantic: 20" to the inside fork   **EDIBILITY:** Excellent

LIMIT: 10 per harvester per day, not to exceed 60 per vessel

TACKLE: A lightweight 20 lb spinning set up, and an 30 lb leader to a #7 J hook. Or, 30 lb leader to small blue / pink trolling lures and #7 J hook. Pre rig a dozen 50 lb leaders with ballyhoo, perfection knot to snap swivel. *YouTube: How to rig ballyhoo. There are great techniques with pin rigs and rubber bands, or J hooks, skirted or naked. Google: Poveromo, naked ballyhoo rig*

FISHING TECHNIQUE: While cruising offshore waters, look for birds. Stabilized 14x40 binoculars are a huge assist. Troll natural baits such as ballyhoo on lightweight spinning rods and 20 lb mono. Bi-mini twist on end of main line to swivel clip at end. 50 lb leader with a 7/0 J hook, rigged (a variety of ways) to a bare ballyhoo dead or alive. Place two other rods with a 50 lb leader and lures from transom one at surface, one below. If a 20"+ keeper, leave it in the water. Have plenty of ballyhoo chunks at the ready and multiple "pitch rods" with 30 lb leader and 5/0 to 7/0 J hooks. Or, a bucktail.

OUTING & TACTIC

Captain Jimmy and I went out in search of dolphin fish, aka mahi mahi. It proved to be a master class in catching. By days end, we had 23 in the box. Dolphin can be found from 10 to 30 miles offshore, in waters 200' to 1000'+ deep – so you may have some ground to cover, or – not. Stabilized binoculars (and a tuna tower) is a giant assist, rather than to aimlessly troll.

Before you troll aimlessly for hours on end, look for birds that are low to the water and circling. Don't go right up to the birds. Instead, try to cut off the dolphin cruising the Gulf Stream. You have to imagine that the dolphin are cruising up stream, or west to east. Once you have birds in the area, and hopefully a good weed line, place two bare ballyhoo on your outriggers. Let them out 150'. You can also put two skirt artificial lures out 100' from your transom. Make your own with 1/2 oz egg sinkers. Troll east to west, and northwest.

If you come upon some debris, it is the gift that keeps on giving. You might see dozens of migrating dolphin around something as small as a bucket. Keep moving slowly around the debris, in a 100' circle. Toss in prepared chunks of ballyhoo, then a whole ballyhoo on a lightweight spinning rod and bare hook. *Two things to note: Reel the ballyhoo or pinfish back to the boat at a pretty good clip, so jacks don't get it. Once the dolphinfish takes your bait, open the bail and let it eat the bait. Then, after a few seconds, start reeling in. This is the difference between catching and getting bit off – let it eat the bait.*

As Capt. Jimmy says, people over think dolphin fishing. The common mistake is using too heavy gear. *"You don't need 50 lb braid to bring in a 15 lb fish,"* he might say. You don't necessarily need a skirt over your ballyhoo either. It is a preference, not a rule. As for the leader, 50-80 lb fluoro with a loop knot for the clip, and a 7/0 hook on the end. As for the ballyhoo rig, there are so many including pre-rigged. I like a basic pin rig and rubberband. I also like a pin rig with a chin weight and copper wire. Then there is the chain rig that sits further back in the anal cavity. YouTube each of these and decide what you like. Have 6 -12 at the ready in tupperware on ice per two angler 1/2 day to 3/4 day outing. Bring 1/2 dozen plastics along too.

TIPS & TARGETING WITH CAPTAIN JIMMY GAGLIARDINI

BLACKFIN TUNA

© Diane Rome Peebles

SIZE: Common 20 to 28 inches

HABITAT: Coastal to offshore waters, wrecks, humps, 200'+ depth

MIN LENGTH: None   **EDIBILITY:** Excellent / sushi grade

LIMIT: 2 fish per angler per day, or 10 fish per boat / 5 anglers

TACKLE: 5500 spinning rod, 30 - 50 lb leader, 5/0 - 7/0 J hook

BAIT: Live pinfish, live pilchards, live or cut ballyhoo, cedar plug Small feathered blue/pink lures work well too, and surface poppers.

FISHING TECHNIQUE: Troll at 5 knots, or bottom fish with live pinfish.

VENTING TECHNIQUE: When you fish in water 50' to 200'+ deep, you will require a venting tool or descending device. It is likely that you will not want to keep a greater amberjack, in which case you don't want to kill it. Its bladder fills with air, aka barotrauma, a condition caused when fish are brought up from waters deeper than 50'. You have to help release this air. *YouTube: How to use a venting tool on fish*. It might take a few attempts. If you don't have a venting tool, lay the fish down and press or gently push down just below the ribs. Also *Google: How to use a descending device / YouTube.*

OUTING & TACTIC

Captain Jimmy and I went out in search of blackfin tuna. We combined this outing with dolphinfish fishing. Our first destination was a well known area off of Marathon FL, called **The Marathon Humps**.

Approximately 25 miles offshore, The Humps is an area 1200' deep, where an 800' underwater mountain rises, making it 400' deep. The area is home to a wide variety of fish including blackfin tuna, dolphinfish, greater amberjack, and marlin. But, blackfin tuna can be found in shallower depths too, of 150' - 250' as you surface troll. Captain Jimmy demonstrated that you don't need sport fishing gear, or a heavy duty rod and reel to target tuna and dolphinfish. In fact, he uses his lightweight spinning rods on 20 lb mono for trolling. I was taken aback at first, but in fact, that is all you need.

To compensate for extra strength, Capt. Jimmy uses a Bimini twist at the end of the base mono, then ties his 4' - 50 lb leader on with a Bristol or Albright knot. The two transom rods, 75' back get artificials with a 4/0 circle hook, while the two outriggers, 150' back get bare ballyhoo, have a 60 lb to 80 lb leader trolled at 6 knots. Since we are targeting blackfin tuna first, we attach a 4' length of 40 lb leader to the 50 lb leader. Afterward, when we're ready to target dolphinfish, we cut off the 40 lb leader, and go with the 50 lb leader. If we don't have luck trolling, we look for something on the sonar, or just go to the area that seems to have action. We slowly drop down a live pinfish using 25' of 30 lb fluoro leader. At the knot, we place a small split shot weight solely as a preventer for our 8 oz egg sinker. The sinker is attached to 12" of 20 lb fluoro, and a snap swivel – to slide, but not past the weight. In this case we up the hook to 5/0.

Another popular technique to target blackfin tuna is by livebaiting handfuls of pilchards at regular 30 second intervals. Catch lots of pilchards by day and fish the hours either side of sunset. In the 175' range, anchored or adrift, toss the bait in to attract the tuna. When the tuna surface, toss in more live bait, then freeline or cast back a pilchard on a 2/0+ circle hook, and 30 lb+ leader – and catch. Another traditional method is a basic bottom rig: 5 oz+ sinker, 30' leader, and 3/0+ circle hook with live bait. Try this at different depths.

TIPS & TARGETING WITH CAPTAIN JIMMY GAGLIARDINI
WAHOO

© Diane Rome Peebles

SIZE: Common 20 to 30 pounds – to over 100 lb; maximum potential up to 98 inches

HABITAT: Offshore waters; generally solitary, 200' - 700'

FISHING TECHNIQUE: Early morning. Wahoo are caught by trolling bait and artificial lures on flatlines. Surface trolling is sometimes effective, but deep trolling is much more likely to produce a wahoo.

MIN LENGTH: None

LIMIT: 2 per day

EDIBILITY: Excellent / sushi grade

TACKLE: Light to medium ocean trolling outfits with lines up to 50 lb test; 80 lb isn't too heavy for good sport with big specimens. Even 100 lb+ for diving lures. Some are caught by deep jigging. A wire leader is recommended with wahoo lure and live bait presentation.

BAIT: Most productive bait is a weighted feather or similar trolling lure, rigged in combination with a whole skirted ballyhoo. A down rigger or planer, to get your bait down 30' is a good approach. Wahoo have been known to grab surface baits too. *Google: Wahoo fishing.*

OUTING & TACTIC

Wahoo are fast fish. They are most often caught while trolling fast. Instead of the common 5 knots speed, it is recommended to troll between 10 and 12 knots for targeting wahoo. Diving lures e.g., Nomad 2000, 2200 and others are recommended. Also recommended when using $50+ lures, heavier 100 lb - 200 lb leader and wire. Wahoo are generally solitary creatures, except during a full moon. In instances of full moon, they school, making the odds for catch more favorable. Another important factor, as with many fish is water temperature. For wahoo it is 68 to 78 degrees.

Dolphinfish and wahoo can be targeted in the same 200' - 700' waters. But, wahoo tend to be found deeper in the water column, say 30' to 50' down, so a down rigger or planer is a great assist. You can catch wahoo while targeting dolphinfish, going 5 knots and surface plugging, but it is more a result of good fortune. Like dolphinfish, wahoo are attracted to ballyhoo as well. Aside from a down rigger or planer, there are a variety of in line trolling weights too. If you are fortunate enough to land a big wahoo, you might need to circle around the fish a number of times as you reel it in.

Note regarding offshore fishing: It is around the 14 mile mark that you lose your cell service, so no calling anyone, not even TowBoatUS. You can't use your VHF radio either unless another boat is nearby, because it is antenna to antenna able, or line of sight only. You lose your FM radio too, when you lose cell service – just to give you an idea. And, you can't anchor either where it is 1000'+ deep. Good thing that you left a float plan with a loved one and instructed him or her to call someone if you don't return by a certain time. These are things that many people don't consider, but it is all a part of the 4-C philosophy – caution, common sense, consideration and communication. Good thing that you got in the habit of wearing a PFD, right? And, that you have an EPIRB or SPOT with you, electronic beacon devices to call for help in the instance of life or death situations. SPOT is device for both message and SOS. Granted, this spread might be equally about offshore considerations and wahoo. But, when you take proper precaution and save a life by carrying a tracking device, you might just say – woo-hoo!

TIPS & TARGETING

SPINY LOBSTER

© Diane Rome Peebles

HABITAT: Ocean and Gulf sides. Often found under ledges, and in holes. Lobster hide during the day and forage at night.

TECHNIQUE: Lobster are caught in a variety of ways; commercial lobstermen use traps. Some use scuba, and others use bully net boats (see below). Recreationally, people use a tickle stick, gloves, and a net. Some use scuba and / or hookah.

MIN LENGTH: Carapace (from eyes to tail) must be larger than 3"

LIMIT: 6 per person per day recreational catch

RECIPE: Cut tail down center, BBQ at 500° for ten minutes, butter.

BULLY NET BOAT: A boat with its helm at the extreme bow, lights in the water, and livewell in the center of the boat. Bully net lobster people night time fish in 2' to 4' of water while lobster are foraging. Bully netters use a net that is perpendicular to the pole and pounce the lobster from above. Commercial catch can be as many as 250 per night. A recreational bully netter is only allowed 6 per person. Remember to check the **Fish Rules** app each time that you go out.

OUTING & TACTIC

Florida Keys spiny lobster, aka bugs, unlike Maine lobster, have no claws. Lobstering is a huge economic driver, and not just for tourism. Commercial lobstering translates into millions of dollars every year. The recreational lobster catch is a great experience but it is not easy, especially if free diving without the aid of a scuba tank or hookah rig. *Use of a ski tow rope is the norm here, to save energy.*

If you are not a regular snorkeler, it is recommended that you spend a day or so acclimating your body to the rigors of the lobster chase; holding your breath under water, and climbing in and out of a boat several times a day. If you add current and seagrass to the mix, the degree of difficulty is multiplied. If you wish to eat lobster for dinner, you should probably hire a guide. *Note: Scuba and hookah is legal but it is also expensive, so the majority of people snorkel / free dive.*

Catching a lobster is fun, but first you have to find them. Once you do, use the tickle stick – delicately. You only want to coax the lobster out of its hiding hole, not harm it. Next, return to the surface for air. Then, go back down and position your net behind the bug, without scaring it – lobster are fast! Once in the net, stick your gloved hand into the net and grab a hold of it. Most lobsters are found in channels, where grass meets sand, at bridge pilings, and around rocky surfaces. As for depth, start at 3' to 4', then try a little deeper, but only if you are able to. Make sure that the lobster's carapace, between the eyes to the start of the tail, does not fit within the measuring gauge. Take this measurement while in the water.

Always check for females carrying eggs. We don't keep those. We come to terms with the ugly part of taking a life, knowing that if we don't millions of tourists, commercial fishermen, and recreational locals – will. And, if we reason that we will never take more than we legally should, and always follow the rules, good karma happens. As for me, I take far less than I am legally permitted to, 1/1000th less in fact. Even though I am permitted 6 lobster per day, I am more likely to take that amount per month. If it bothers you to take a life, release it. The activity alone is fun – and good exercise.

TIPS & TARGETING

TARPON

© Diane Rome Peebles

SIZE: Up to 8 feet (50 to 150 lbs and larger)

HABITAT: Primarily inshore fish; adults spawn offshore. Tarpon are found throughout Florida's coastal environment during the summer months at; bridges, flats, and channels. They migrate through the Keys April through June, and migrate as far north as the Carolinas.

MIN LENGTH: Tarpon more than 40" must remain in the water

LIMIT: 1 per harvester / catch and release   **EDIBILITY:** Poor

TACKLE: Generally a 20 lb to 30 lb or greater, base line braid, and a 40 lb to 80 lb leader with a 7/0 circle hook. The bait is often freelined with a balloon or float to keep the (bridled) bait from dashing to the bottom, and instead, kept up in the water column. While tarpon are not a toothy predator, a long heavy monofilament leader is very important to protect your line from being cut by the gill plate or tail.

BAIT: Tarpon are most often attracted to live bait; blue crabs, pinfish, pilchard, mullet, and grunt to name a few. But, artificial lures can work well too. It is wise to replace any treble hook lure with a single hook. It makes it easier to take the hook out, and helps to protect the fish. *YouTube: How to bridle bait for tarpon fishing.*

OUTING & TACTIC

There is not enough room on two pages to tell you how to properly target tarpon. It is the same with all fish actually. But, there is always YouTube. I didn't expect YouTube to become such an integral part of this book, but I am glad that it has for a couple of reasons: 1) It gives the book a social media presence that is more in tune with the times. And, 2) It is a great way to learn. As I made mention in the dedication, without YouTube, *"I would not know how to maintain a motor, much less tie a knot."* But, nothing replaces hands-on experience. You have to get out there and do it – to learn hands-on.

Many of you, no doubt, have already invested a lot of time and money into learning how to fish. It takes a while to fully understand things like: bait presentation, go where the fish are, fish when they feed, and use what they eat advice. One word in particular plays a vital role. And, that word is – desire. I have laid out my battles with learning how to fish throughout the years. There were many an occasion where I wanted to give up on fishing all together. But, I had the desire to learn. After all, fishing and boating is a way of life here in the Keys. It is, in fact, Keys culture; life on the water, boating, diving, and fishing. This book – was a way for me to archive my experiences, and to share information that will (hopefully) help you understand fishing better, both here and where you live.

Captain Jimmy does offer tarpon charter trips, but we didn't get a chance to go out together. So, I am going to break from my normal "how to catch" advice and instead tell you someone who can explain it better than I can. And, I am happy it worked out this way. Go to the YouTube channel, **Key West Kayak Fishing**. Steve has five videos on the subject of targeting tarpon called, **Beginners Guide To Catching A Florida Keys Tarpon**.

Of course, there is no replacing catching by doing, and I urge you to. And, if this is your first experience or your 100th backcountry fishing in the Keys, try doing so out of the Lower Keys and specifically, Surgarloaf Marina. It just doesn't get more beautiful than here. For those of you who do not interact with the online world, let me scratch the surface here and tell you where to begin.

TIPS & TARGETING

YOUR FL KEYS BACKCOUNTRY GUIDE: TARPON, PERMIT, BONEFISH
Captain Dustin Huff: Marathon, FL - 305-360-1404
Captain Gabe Nyblad: Little Torch Key - 989-339-0931
Capt Chris Robinson: Cudjoe Gardens - 305-304-5498
Captain Tim Carlile: Sugarloaf Marina - 305-304-4834
Captain Aaron Snell: Big Coppitt Key / Key West - 305-304-0261
Captain Will Benson: Key West - 305-923-6114

WHEN: very early morning around sunrise, or an hour either side of sunset, and night time too. These are the best times for most all fishing – not when it is convenient for you, but when the fish are feeding. Rig: 20 lb to 30 lb braid, 40 lb to 80 lb leader, and a 7/0 circle hook. You want maximum line capacity as these silver kings can take you for a 30 minute or more ride. A balloon or float rig is used to keep your bait up in the water column and appear natural.

WHERE: You want to scout places where there is good current, and some depth too, where water flows from the Gulf side to the ocean side. Flats fishing for tarpon while poling in open water is definitely a more organic experience. In both instances, watch for tarpon rolling on the surface. I always keep a lookout for professional flats boat guides to make note of where they fish. I might want to try that spot another day, but I want to stay clear of them too.

BAIT: Live bait, blue crab, mullet, pilchard, pinfish and grunt.

HOW: Anchor in a channel or under a bridge and freeline. Some anglers use chum, while others use shrimp boat bi-catch, and freeline similar bait on a 7/0 hook with a balloon 10' to 15' from the hook.

During this "special" backcountry technique of tarpon fishing, your guide will sight fish with the sun at his / her back, and will alert you when and where to cast. Everything is subtle except for your pounding heart as you ready yourself to bow to the silver king. When tarpon take your bait, you lower the tip of your rod, or "bow." Tarpon are skittish, you want to stay low and keep noise and movement to a minimum – even when closing hatches.

OUTING & TACTIC

Live bait and artificial both work well on the flats, as do spinning set-ups and fly rods. To learn more about tarpon visit this website, *bonefishtarpontrust.org*. This is a great organization that you should definitely check out before you fish for tarpon. And, if you can, donate as well.

So, four take-aways: 1) Hire a local guide, 2) Go to the fish, 3) Fish when they feed, and 4) Use what they eat. Tarpon like a water temperature in the 70° - 75° range, but these are the larger migrating tarpon. The smaller resident tarpon are here year round. When: on the ocean side, the migration season starts around mid April and goes through June. In the backcountry, play the tides. Be sure to check out **Jose Wejebe's** videos at *spanishflytv.com*. One such video is on the palolo worm hatch in late May, early June.

Tarpon love palolo worms. It is a fascinating phenomenon. Tarpon, bonefish, and permit fishing is in the "bucket list" category of fishing. Many anglers from around the globe come to the Florida Keys and pay good money to catch tarpon, and all three – to live the dream. Here in the Lower Keys, there is something known as the grand slam of fishing – it is catching a tarpon, bonefish, and a permit on the same outing, or on the same consecutive days of your charter.

The palolo hatch is especially exciting. The worms make their run to the reef during an outgoing tide around the full moon. Best fishing happens around sunset and in light to no wind. These 1" to 2" worms sort of cork screw their way with the outgoing tide. The tarpon celebrate in clear sight. But, it is difficult to actually get their attention. Sometimes you have to go a larger bait because they are so fixated by the worms for – protein, buzz, nip, or whatever it might be. You just have to come down and see it for yourself. It is certain to be an experience that you will not soon forget. In fact, it might just keep you coming down year after year.

All local guides have one singular common goal. It is the hope that we are but one highlight of your Florida Keys visit. Happy fishing!

Q & A

FISHING Q&A

I use this **Q&A** to answer many of the fishing questions you might have. Streamline your effort to a few spots and a few species at first. Fish the bridges, patch reef, reef, and beyond. Happy Fishing!

1. **What tackle shop can you recommend?**
   Lower Keys Tackle on Big Pine Key, West Marine, The Tackle Box in Marathon, Cudjoe Sales, and Key West Bait & Tackle

2. **What rod and reel should I buy?**
   I like Penn rods and reels for novice to seasoned anglers. But, there are many brands out there. Look into the Penn Spinfisher series rod and reel combo; 4500, 5500 are two good reels. Shimano, Fin Noir, and BG reels are good too.

3. **What do I need in my tackle box?**
   Get a couple of plastic containers with dividers for hooks, swivels, beads and the like. Weighted jig heads are great, but you want a good supply of weights and hooks too. Tackle adds up fast. Start small – with one box and some 1/0 to 4/0 hooks, #2 and #4 hooks, and 1 oz to 3 oz egg sinkers. Buy a pack of swivels and beads, a scissor and or nail clipper. See the complete list on page 131. If you like artificial lures, try some Gulp brand shrimp, and DOA lures.

4. **Spinning reel versus Conventional reel set up?**
   A spinning reel is generally intended for casting, but it is versatile, and a better rod for beginners. The conventional rod and reel is a good rod for bottom fishing, jigging, and trolling.

5. **What other accessories do you recommend?**
   A button-less long sleeve quick dry SPF fishing shirt, a neck gaiter, a visor, sunscreen, and polarized sunglasses. You also want a cooler, and frozen water bottles – rather than ice.

6. **Should I use braid or monofilament?**
   Braid or monofilament is up to the individual. Mono stretches ⅓ of its length and is more forgiving for the novice angler. Braid has no stretch, so we generally add a 25' mono top shot to it with an FG knot. Then, the leader. Braid is much finer so you can get a lot more line on the spool. Mono is certainly more affordable, and quieter. If trolling - mono.

Note: If you use mono, it's a good idea to let out 100' or so with nothing on it – no hook, and let it drag behind the boat on your way out, so to stretch it out and rid the spool memory. Then, there is line strength. For spinning reels, start with 15 and 20 lb. Another outfit might be 30 lb braid with 30 to 50 lb leader depending what you are targeting e.g., mutton snapper. If yellowtail fishing, start with 12 lb Ande mono, and 12 lb Gama or Diamond fluoro leader – and a #4 hook.

7. **What pound test fluorocarbon should I use?**
    I like to have a variety of fluorocarbon leaders. For smaller, snapper and the like, start with Gama 10 lb to 12 lb. But, have 15 lb to 20 lb, 30 lb and 40 lb to round out your supply.

8. **How do I know what type and size hook to use?**
    Go to a good tackle shop and ask for a variety of hooks for 1 and 2 pound snapper, to 8 pound jacks, and 20 pound grouper or similar, and see what they say. It will be something like #2 and #4 hooks for yellowtail, and 2/0, to 7/0 for other.

9. **How can I catch bait?**
    There are several ways to catch bait. Purchase a pinfish trap and bait it with a 1/2 block of chum, or an entire block.
    Note: Do not use a power saw to cut the chum. It is a mess that you are sure to regret. Instead, use a breaker bar and a strong 3 lb hammer. If you get hooked on fishing, you might want to invest in a 6' to 8' + cast net for baitfish and minnows. I recommend a fine 3/8" mesh net. Otherwise, you will be picking minnows out of the mesh for a good while. Your boat should have a livewell. You can also try a #12 hook on 8 lb leader with a bit of squid on it for pinfish and ballyhoo.

10. **Where do we go if we don't catch fish?**
    Low Key Fisheries on Cudjoe Key, right across from Cudjoe Sales has a great selection of fresh caught fish. They also offer a good selection of bait, chum, oats and more. Another option, just up the road – **The Square Grouper** restaurant.

11. **What's a typical rig for: bottom fishing, freelining?**
    Make your presentation as low profile as possible, no swivel for freelining, just line to line and a small #4 hook for yellowtail. If bottom fishing, again line to line, and then a jig, or a Carolina rig: weight, swivel, leader, and hook.

12. **How do I know what weight to use?**

    If no current, no weight, or a light weight jig. As the current increases, so does the weight / jig head: 1/16 oz to 1/4 oz to 1/2 oz, or Carolina / Knocker rig 1 oz, 2 oz, and as much as 12 oz depending on species, depth, and current.

13. **What is a Knocker rig?**

    A Knocker rig is an alternative to a Carolina rig in that the egg sinker sits right atop your hook, perhaps with a bead in between. You lower the Knocker rig to the bottom, and add a couple of feet of slack. With a Carolina rig, lift the weight off the bottom a bit. The Carolina rig leader can be 4' or 25'+.

14. **Where do I go to find fish?**

    The million dollar question. In general, fish like structure rocks, bridges, humps, and holes. Look at your GPS sonar for jagged edges, and fish too. Check out CMOR and Navionics Vision Pro. Try the patch reef 25' to 45'. Anchor over sand, and chum back to the dark spots, aka patch reef.

15. **How do I know what legal size and limit is?**

    The app, Fish Rules is a great way to identify, see size, limit, and open/closed season. It is necessary to have a tape (sticker) with a ruler on your boat too. If not, for reference, a 5 gallon bucket is 12" across.

16. **What is a good cast net to purchase?**

    Any fine mesh net is what I recommend. But, be careful around debris and branches so not to tear your net. Start small with a 6' net, and work your way up. Go to YouTube to learn how to throw it and see what works best for you. Fine mesh 3/16" nets are more expensive than 3/8" net, twice as much, and twice the weight, but worth it. Note: Don't wear a shirt with buttons. Go to: boatingmag.com/choosing-cast-net.

17. **How do I know what fish to target?**

    Depending on where you live – is the place to start. Find out what's running and when. Check the water temperature. Look at Tides4Fishing.com. Check the wind and current. In some places it is striped bass and others – walleye. It could be mackerel, snapper, or mahi. Check the open season for a particular species. Fortunately in the Keys, there is a wide variety of fish to target. Sometimes you get surprised and land a cobia or mutton snapper when yellowtail fishing. Try to get to a point where you can target a particular species. Until then, just be happy to catch anything, even a tan.

18. **What tide will produce best results?**
Again, depends where and what. If at a bridge, some people believe, slack to incoming. Others like an outgoing tide. The online charts recommend a low tide at the bridges, and high tide in the backcountry. If at the reef, you want a decent current where you can fish off the stern of your boat, so that your chum slick is sending out a message, "Here fishy!"

19. **Is the tide table accurate?**
In general yes and no. Check the tide for yourself. Make a visual note of the time when the tide turns versus what the tide chart says. If strong current, the chart tends to be off as much as an hour or two. Strong and light currents, especially at bridges, generally increases each month by the day.

20. **Are there easier ways to catch bait?**
There is something called a Sabiki rig which requires no bait and – works. You can put an hour aside and catch pinfish using a #4 hook, or a small jig, with a tiny piece of squid on it. Have a bucket with an aerator to put them in. You might catch 12 to 24 in this time. Use chum.

21. **Any other advice that you can recommend?**
Yes, only take your limit, if that – enough for dinner. Only take legal. Make sure that you are informed. Don't play dumb. Approach fishing as karma. Fines are steep.

22. **How do I tie wire to a: swivel, lure, hook, line?** Purchase a package of #3 wire (to start) for mackerel. And, #4 for king mackerel. Google: Haywire twist / YouTube. Practice. Wire is only required for toothy fish, mackerel, barracuda, shark, and wahoo to name a few. Always have BandAids available.

23. **What are the best knots, and best way to learn them?**
As with everything this book – YouTube (and practice). Reminder: Uni knot (line to line), Advanced clinch knot (line to hook), Bimini twist (makes base line 2x's stronger), Palomar knot (line to hook), Loop knot, (for jigs and live bait), Bristol knot, (leader to Bimini) These are the most common knots used for saltwater fishing.

24. **Is it OK to head offshore, 25+ miles out alone?**

    Actually, not especially advised. There is already a lot at risk going offshore: no cell service, too deep to anchor, and potential for weather change. Why go it alone? You are also likely trolling while offshore. Trolling requires a minimum of two people to do it right: set the outriggers, reel in the fish while the boat is underway. Then, to gaff said fish. Tough to do alone. It's best to have a fishing buddy or two. And, having two outboards is always better than one, when going far offshore.

25. **Which guide should I choose in the Lower Keys?**

    There are many great Lower Keys guides to get you on the water. The answer really depends on the following: Where are you staying? What kind of fishing do you want to do? And, how experienced are you? Go with the best you can find because you will be spending a pretty penny, $650 - $850+ for a half day 4 hrs, and more for a full day. I recommend **Captain Jimmy Gagliardini** *and High Caliber Sportfishing Charters for offshore and inshore fishing charters in the Marathon, FL area.* **Captain Jimmy***, 305-395-0915 caters to the novice and seasoned angler alike – and families too. For a good variety of recreational tours, including; eco, sandbar, snorkel, paddleboard, fishing, sunset, and hands-on boat lessons – I recommend* **Captain Brian** *of* **Keys Boat Tours** *(.com) and 305-699-7166. They operate out of Big Pine Key RV at MM 33. There is* **Captain Troy Phillipps** *out of Big Pine Key 305-395-4729,* **Captain Larry White***, 305-393-4153 is a long time local who can teach you to navigate the backcountry like no other. He offers fishing charters too. For the motion sensitive, Ryan of* **LandBoat Charters***, 305-204-9772, can help you with bridge fishing.* **Captain Jim Sharpe***, 305-745-1530, hosts the longest running fishing show,* **This Week In Fishing,** *every Thursday at 6PM on 104.1 radio. Co-hosts include* **Captain Tim Carlile** *and* **Donna Hart***, manager of* **Lower Keys Tackle** *on Big Pine Key.* **Captain Tim***, 305-304-4834 is a renowned flats fishing specialist who can put you onto bonefish, tarpon, and permit while showing you some beautiful backcountry scenery too. Captain Tim operates out of the spectacularly Keysz* **Sugarloaf Marina** *at MM 17, just 20 minutes drive from Key West.*

GLOSSARY

3-Point turn: The standard method of turning a vehicle around to face the opposite direction in a limited space, using forward and reverse gears.

4-C's: Caution, common sense, consideration of others, and communication.

Aboard: On a boat.

Aft: Towards the stern, or back of boat.

Adrift: Floating loose, not on moorings, anchor or towline.

Advanced (Improved) Clinch knot: One of the most widely used fishing knots. It provides a good method of securing fishing line to a hook, lure, or swivel. Often used to fasten a leader to a hook.

Aggregate bag limit: Similar to "bag limit," aggregate bag limit applies to individual anglers and are only used on similar species such as grouper or snapper and are managed by FWC.

Aground: When a boat hull is touching the bottom of the sea bed.

Aid to Navigation (ATON): Lighthouses, lights, buoys, electronic aids, sound signals, radio beacons, and other markers on land and sea that specifically intend to help navigate, or warn of danger or obstructions.

Albright knot: A bend used in angling. It is a strong knot used to tie two different diameters of line together, for instance to tie fluorocarbon to braid. The Albright is relatively smooth and passes through guides when required.

Amidship: In or toward center of the boat.

Anchor: A heavy object attached to a rope or chain used to moor a vessel to the sea bottom, typically having a ring at one end and curved and barbed flukes at the other.

Apparent wind: The direction and velocity of wind as felt in a moving boat.

Aquaplaning device: Any type of device the you can use to skim on the surface of the water, i.e., boat, water skis, jet skis.

Astern: toward the stern / rear of the boat.

Back fire flame arrestor: a device attached to an engine's carburetor that prevents a fire from leaving the carburetor system in the event of a backfire; equipped for all gasoline engines.

Bag limit: A law imposed on fishermen restricting the number of fish within a specific species or group of species they may kill and keep.

Baitfish: Small fish used as bait to catch a larger fish.

Barometer: An instrument for measuring air pressure.

Barotrauma: A condition experienced by some deep water fish that are brought quickly to the surface. Fish experiencing barotrauma often sustain serious injuries, and upon release, are unable to swim or dive back to depth.

Beam: Width of a boat at its widest point.

Beam reach: *(Sailing)* This is a precise point of sail and is exactly perpendicular (or 90°) to the direction of the wind, from the direction of the wind. Generally for most boats this is an efficient point of sail and can provide for the fastest speeds.

Bearing: The direction to an object, given as a horizontal angle from a line of reference.

Bend: To attach a line to another line. Also, to attach a line to a spar or stay.

Bernoulli's Principle: One very small piece of a large mathematical theory that explains lift. For a sailboat sail, the fluid is air and the "lift" is a horizontal force that propels the boat forward (and also makes it lean). So "lift" doesn't push the boat up, it pushes it forwards and sideways.

Bilge: The internal part of the boat's hull.

Bilge pump: Pump used to clear water or liquid from the bilge.

Bilgeboard: *(Sailing)* A plate in a vertical fore-and-aft plane, that can be lowered through a slot in the bottom of a sailboat to reduce leeway.

Bimini top: A canvas top that creates shade on a boat. Often mounted to the gunwale of a boat, it is capable to fold down flat when not in use.

Bimini twist: A fishing knot considered to be a 100% knot – providing 100% line strength. It creates a double line with a loop at the end to which a leader can be attached with a loop-to-loop connection.

Biodegradable: Capable of being broken down into harmless products.

Bitter end: the inboard end of a rope or cable.

Blood knot: A bend knot most used for joining sections of monofilament line together. A Blood knot will maintain a high portion of the line's inherent strength.

Blue Star: A program established by Florida Keys National Marine Sanctuary recognizing tour operators who are committed to promoting responsible and sustainable diving, snorkeling, and fishing practices to reduce the impact of these activities on ecosystems in the Florida Keys.

Boat hook: A pole with a blunt hook to facilitate line handling.

Boom: *(Sailing)* The boom is the horizontal pole which extends from the bottom of the mast. Adjusting the boom towards the direction of the wind is how the sailboat is able to harness wind power in order to move forward or backwards.

Bow: Forward or front part of boat.

Bowline: A knot used to form a loop that neither slips or jams.

Braid: One of the earliest types of fishing line, made of woven fibers. Braided lines have 1/3 to 1/4 the diameter of mono or fluorocarbon lines. Therefore, it is easy to fit much longer braided line on a spool than mono or fluoro line for the same strength.

Bridge clearance: Distance from waterline to a boat's highest point.

Bristol knot: A low-profile connection that is useful for joining the double line of a Bimini twist, Spider hitch or similar loop knot to a heavier piece of monofilament.

Bulkhead: Transverse wall in a boat that usually bears weight and supplies hull support.

Buoy: A floating aid to navigation, defined by color and shape, which is anchored at a given position.

Can buoy: Green cylindrical buoys with odd numbers that are positioned on the left side of channels when returning from sea. Green squares with odd numbers are the equivalent of can buoys.

Capacity plate: A placard required on all boats; lists the maximum weight capacity for the boat as well as the horsepower rating.

Capsize: To tip over.

Carolina rig: A bait rig with the weight fixed above the hook, instead of sliding down to it, i.e., Knocker rig. The Carolina rig is designed catch bottom feeding fish.

Catamaran: A boat with two hulls that are connected by a deck.

Centerboard: *(Sailing)* A keel-like pivoting device, typically in a trunk, that can be lowered or raised to act as a keel.

Chalk: A metal fitting, on the boat, through which the anchor or mooring lines are led through.

Chart: A map that shows the characteristics of a body of water: includes navigational aids, hazards to navigation such as reefs or shoals and water depths.

Chart plotting: the art of laying a safe course, fixing the position and reassuring that position, while steering the ship on that course.

Chicken rig: A quick and easy bottom rig to tie. The rig itself consists of multiple hooks with the weight on the bottom. It presents bait vertically in the water column, great for schooling fish suspended near the bottom.

Chine: The area of a vessel's hull where the bilge angles up to become the topsides of the hull.

Chum: Bait consisting of fish parts, fish oil, bone and blood. Chum comes in frozen blocks, also known as *"stink bait."*

Chumming: The process of scattering fish scraps in the water as bait to attract fish to your designated spot and stimulate feeding. The stink bait draws both bait species and your target species that will consume both the baitfish and your chum. For certain species, this technique is essential to success.

Circle hook: A type of fish hook which is sharply curved back in a circular shape. It has become widely used among anglers because the hook generally catches more fish and is rarely swallowed.

Cleat: A fitting to which lines are made fast.

Cleat hitch: A quick and easy method of tying a rope to a cleat on a dock or boat that is also easy to untie.

Clew: *(Sailing)* The after, lower corner of the sail.

Close hauled: *(Sailing)* Sailing as close to the No Sail Zone as possible without entering it. The sails of the boat will be in tight.

Close reach: *(Sailing)* Includes any angle to the wind between close hauled and a beam reach. Sails are let out more than close hauled.

Clove hitch: A hitch for temporarily fastening a line to a spar, post or piling.

Come about: *(Sailing)* To tack or change heading relative to the wind.

Compass: An instrument for determining direction.

Cuddy: A small shelter cabin in a boat.

Current: An ocean current is a continuous, directed movement of sea water generated by a number of forces acting upon the water, including wind, the Coriolis effect, breaking waves, and temperature and salinity differences.

Daggerboard: *(Sailing)* A plate in a vertical fore-and-aft plane, that can be lowered through a slot in the bottom of a sailboat to reduce leeway.

Danforth anchor: A patented lightweight anchor characterized by long narrow twin flukes pivoted at one end of the long shank.

Davits: Mechanical arms extending over the side or stern of a vessel, or over a seawall, to raise or lower a smaller boat.

Dead ahead: Your compass bearing relative to the position of your bow and the direction it is pointing.

Dead reckoning: The process of calculating your current position by using a previously determined position, or fix, and advancing that position based upon known or estimated speeds over elapsed time and course.

Deep-v hull: A hull design that is the shape of a "v." These hulls plane well and through the addition of an engine with greater horsepower, can produce a comfortable ride.

Digital Selective Calling (DSC): A maritime distress and safety call system that allows VHF radios to send an automated Mayday to alerts the US Coast Guard.

Dinghy: A small open boat, often used as a tender for a larger boat.

Displacement hull: A hull designed to move water in a way where it plows through it versus plane over it, e.g., trawler design

Documentation: A special federal license for a vessel.

Draft: The vertical depth measured on a boat from the waterline to the lowest part of the hull.

Emergency Position Indicating Radio Beacon (EPIRB): A device to alert search and rescue services (SAR) in case of an emergency out at sea. It transmits a signal on a specified band to locate a lifeboat, life raft, ship or people in distress.

Engine, four-cycle: An engine that requires two revolutions of its internal parts to complete the internal combustion process.

Engine, two-cycle: An engine that requires one revolution of its internal parts to complete the internal combustion process.

Fall off: *(Sailing)* Falling off is the opposite of heading up. It refers to turning away from the wind. Any time you pull the tiller away from the sail (and towards yourself), your boat will begin to fall off.

Fathom: A nautical measure of length, 6 feet, used for measuring water depth and length of anchor rode.

Fender: An inflated rubber bumper used to protect a boat gunwale against pilings, docks, and areas with big tidal changes.

FG Knot: A popular leader knot. It is very strong and once learned it is an easy and fast method of connecting a leader to your main line. It is absolutely reliable in all classes of line and can be used with mono, braid and fluorocarbon.

Fish safe landing net: A rubber net puts less stress on a fish and increases their chances of survival after being caught. A fish's skin is protected by mucus. Thin knotted string and nylon net bags remove a lot of mucus. Smooth rubber nets remove much less.

Fishfinder: Electronic device that uses sonar to locate and display fish on a monitor.

Fishing leader: A short strand of tough fishing line (often stronger and/or less visible than the main line, i.e., fluorocarbon) that is placed in between the main line in the reel and the hook or lure that an angler is using.

Fishing main line: The bulk of fishing line on the spool of a fishing reel, monofilament, braid, fluorocarbon. A leader is usually tied between the main line and the hook or lure.

Figure eight knot: A stopper knot that helps in sailing by not allowing the tag end of a rope to slip out of it's retaining device, or pulley.

Flat bottom hull: stable type of hull design but provides a bumpy ride when operated at high speeds; a hull that has almost no deadrise.

Flats boat: Type of small, inshore saltwater fishing boat with moderate deadrise and draft, usually equipped with a raised platform aft used by a guide pushing a long pole to silently maneuver the boat through shallow water.

Float plan: A form to be submitted to a local authority or relative on land before leaving port; includes a description of the boat, people onboard, radio and safety equipment carried, and trip plan.

Fluke: The flat palm-shaped or shovel-shaped part of an anchor that digs in to prevent dragging.

Fluorocarbon (Fluoro): This fishing line is mostly used as leader and tied to braid or monofilament. The refractive index of fluorocarbon is close to that of water, making it nearly invisible in water.

Forward: Moving towards the bow of the boat.

Freeboard: The vertical distance measured on a boat from the waterline to the top of the transom.

Freelining: Fishing with live or dead bait and no added weight. Freelining creates a more natural presentation to the bait and is popular for catching speckled trout, and yellowtail snapper.

Furling: *(Sailing)* Rolling or folding a sail on its boom.

Gaff: A stick with a hook or barbed spear, for landing large fish.

Galley: The kitchen area of a boat.

Give-way vessel: The boat that must take immediate and significant action to avoid colliding with another vessel when following the Rules of the Road *(see stand-on vessel)*.

Global Positioning System (GPS): An accurate worldwide navigational and surveying facility based on the reception of signals from an array of orbiting satellites.

Grapnel: A straight, shank anchor with four or five claw-like arms.

Gunwale: The upper edge / top of a boat's sides.

Half hitch: The simplest kind of hitch; a knot made by passing the end of the rope around the rope and then through the loop just made.

Halyard: A line or wire used to hoist a spar, sail or flag.

Hatch: An opening in the boat's deck fitted with a water tight cover.

Haywire twist: Is considered to be the strongest connection for joining wire to a hook, lure or swivel. It can also be used to make a loop in the end of a wire leader. The first twists are called haywire wraps and the second twists are considered barrel wraps.

Head: A marine toilet.

Headway: The forward motion of the boat through the water.

Head to wind: *(Sailing)* Is when the boat is facing directly into the wind. While on a head to wind point of sail the boat will be in the No Sail Zone, the sails will start to flap, and the boat will slow down, eventually starting to drift backwards.

Heave-to: *(Sailing)* To bring the vessel up in position where it will maintain little or no headway, usually with the bow into the wind. To stop.

Head up: *(Sailing)* Heading up refers to turning the bow towards the wind direction. Any time you push the tiller towards the sail (and away from yourself), your boat will begin to head up.

Heeling: *(Sailing)* This is the term for when a sailboat leans over in the water, pushed by the wind.

Helm: The steering wheel controlling the rudder of the boat.

Helmsperson: The person who steers the boat; helmsman.

Horsepower: A unit of power equal, in the US, to 746 watts.

Hull: The body of a boat.

Hull identification number (HIN): A number that includes the manufacturer's identification code, hull serial number, date of certification, and model year, displayed on the boat's hull.

Idle speed: The minimum speed that is necessary to maintain steerage of your vessel.

Impeller: A rubber, neoprene or stainless device within the water pump that pumps water and circulates it though a marine engine.

Imposing silence: A vessel in distress or station control of distress may impose silence on any station that interfere by sending *"Seelonce Mayday."*

Inboard engine: An engine toward the center of a ship, inside the hull.

Intracoastal Waterway (ICW): The ICW is a toll free waterway that is 3000 miles long. It stretches along the Atlantic Coast from Boston, MA to Key West, FL and along the Gulf of Mexico coast from Apalachee Bay, FL to Brownsville, TX.

Irons: *(Sailing)* A sailing vessel is "in irons" when she is trapped in the No Sail Zone, unable to bear away and begin sailing.

Jack plate: A mounting device for an outboard motor that enables operators to vertically raise or lower the motor, thereby controlling propeller depth in the water.

Jibing: *(Sailing)* The opposite of tacking, this basic sailing maneuver refers to turning the stern of the boat through the wind so that the wind changes from one side of the boat to the other side. The boom of a boat will always shift from one side to the other when performing a tack or a jibe. Jibing is a less common technique than tacking, which involves turning a boat directly into the wind.

Keel: The main structural member of a vessel running for and aft; the backbone of a vessel.

Kill switch: A switch with a lanyard that automatically shuts off an engine if disconnected.

King tide: King tides are the highest tides. They are naturally occurring, predictable events. The opposite of a King tide, at low tide, is *Minus tide*.

Knocker rig: Fishing line is tied to a swivel to a leader measuring less than ten feet (five feet is most common). Next, an egg sinker is added to the leader, followed by the hook. When the rig hits the bottom the live bait can swim away from the sinker. Commonly used for grouper fishing.

Knot: A unit of speed on the water that is equal to one nautical mile (6,076 feet) an hour. A fastening made by interweaving rope to form a stopper, to enclose or bind and object, to form a loop or noose.

Latitude: Angular distance north or south of the equator expressed in degrees from 0 to 90, and tabled north or south to indicate the direction of measurement.

Leeward: Located to the side away from the wind.

Line: General term for rope on a boat.

Line of Demarcation: Marks the dividing point between inland and offshore waters.

Livewell: A tank found on fishing boats that is used to keep bait and caught fish alive. It works by pumping fresh water into the tank, as well as keeping the water aerated.

Log: A record of a boat's journey.

Longitude: Distance east to west of the prime meridian expressed degrees 0 to 180 east to west.

Mainsail: The largest regular sail on a sailboat.

Mainsheet: *(Sailing)* The mainsheet (line) is attached to the boom, and is used to control the mainsail. In a rig with no boom on the mainsail, the mainsheet would attach directly to the mainsail clew.

Make fast: To secure a line.

Maritime Mobile Service Identity (MMSI) number: A unique serial number that identifies and individual vessel, a group of vessels, or a coast station. Required for use with digital selective calling equipment.

Mast: Vertical spar that supports sails.

Mayday: The radio distress signal on Channel 16. Mayday (x3) preceded a distress message about grave and imminent danger and request for immediate help. This signal has priority over all other radio calls.

Minus tide: Charts and GPS numbers indicate depth at mean low tide. A Minus tide is when the tide is less than what it says on a chart, often around a full or new moon. The opposite of Minus tide, at high tide, is a *King tide*.

Modified-v hulls: The most common hull for small boats because it combines some of the best characteristics of the other shapes.

Monofilament (Mono): fishing line that is a single strand of material, as opposed to multi-filament lines. Monofilament stretches more than braid or fluorocarbon.

Mooring: A permanent anchor or body that a boat can attach to while in one location.

Multihull: Having one or more hulls; provides more stability and less resistance when moving through the water.

Nautical mile: 6,076 feet, 397 feet longer than a standard mile.

Navigational aid: Any sort of marker which aids the traveler in navigation, usually nautical or aviation travel. Common types of such aids include lighthouses, buoys, fog signals, and day beacons.

Navigable bodies of water: Waterways that are directly connected to the ocean, so are therefore affected by tides and are capable of being navigated by vessels for the purpose of reaching the ocean.

Negligent operation: The operation of a vessel and/or interference with the safe operation of a vessel, so as to endanger lives and/or property.

No discharge zones: Waterway zones in which neither treated or untreated sewage may be released into the water.

No Sail Zone: *(Sailing)* The No Sail Zone is not a point of sail, but an angle, approximately 40° to 45°, either side of the direction of true wind. This zone is where a boat's sails cannot generate any lift and therefore cannot sail. For boats to head up wind they will need to sail a zigzag course using close hauled / reach points of sail.

No-wake speed: Same as idle speed; the minimum speed that is necessary to maintain steerage of your vessel; No waves created by the boat.

Non-motorized vessel: Any vessel that is not mechanically powered by an engine (e.g., sailboats under sail, kayaks, and rowboats).

Nun buoy: Red Buoys with even numbers that are positioned on the right side of channels when returning from sea. Red triangles with even numbers are the equivalent of nun buoys.

Oar: A long paddle used to propel a boat forward.

Onboard: On the boat.

Outboard-powered (Outboard): The engine is mounted outside the hull on the transom.

Outdrive: The propulsion unit on and inboard/outboard or stern drive engine.

Outrigger: A beam, spar, or framework projecting from or over the side of a vessel.

Overboard: Over the side of a boat and into the water.

Palomar knot: A knot used for securing a fishing line to a lure, snap or swivel. It is regarded as one of the strongest and most reliable fishing knots.

Paddle: a short pole with a broad blade at one or both ends, used without an oarlock to move a small boat or canoe through the water.

Pan-Pan: The radio urgency signal, given on Channel 16, announces that there is an urgent matter; used when the safety of a person or vessel is in jeopardy.

Patch reefs: Isolated outcroppings (patches) of coral that are in close proximity to each other but are physically separated by sand. They are typically found in shallow lagoons within a larger collective reef and closer to land.

Peak halyard (Peak): *(Sailing)* is a line that raises the end of a gaff further from the mast, as opposed to the Throat halyard which raises the end nearer to the mast.

Personal flotation device (PFD): A life jacket.

Personal watercraft (PWC): A small motorized vessel powered by a jet drive engine, i.e., Jet Ski.

Pitch: The pitch of a propeller is defined as "the distance a propeller would move in one revolution if it were moving through a soft solid, like a screw through wood."

Pitchpoling: A boat being thrown end over end in rough seas.

Pivot point: A point aft of the bow, forward of the midpoint. A vessel appears to turn at its pivot point.

Planing: A boat is said to be planing when its displacement decreases, it lifts itself over the bow wave, and moves on the top of the water at high speeds.

Port: The left side of the boat as you face forward. A destination or harbor, i.e., when a boat is docked it is in port.

Planing hull: A hull designed to lift out of the water at high speeds.

Position: The actual geographical location of a vessel defined by two parameters called coordinates. Customarily used are latitude and longitude. Position may also be as a bearing and distance from an object.

Powerboat: Any vessel that is mechanically powered by an engine.

Presentation: An effort to present your bait as indistinguishable from nature as possible, as if detached from the line and constantly moving as it ordinarily might, i.e., trolling, freelining, use of long leaders, and the appropriate matching of hook to bait ratio.

Propeller (Prop): A device consisting of a central hub with radiating blades that when turned in the water creates discharge that drives the boat.

Quarter: The sides of the boat aft of amidships.

Radar: Self-contained navigation and collision avoidance system consisting of a shipboard transmitter and receiver.

Radio check: Spoken test call by boater asking what the strength and clarity of the transmission is. A response indicates that the radio is working.

Range: The distance in nautical miles that the vessel can travel with the available fuel onboard.

Ready about: *(Sailing)* Last warning given by a helmsman before tacking and turning the bow into the wind, notifying the crew that the boom and sail will cross the boat.

Red, right, returning: A saying to remember which aids you should be seeing off the vessel's starboard side when return from seaward / the ocean.

Reef safe sunscreen: Made with zinc oxide and titanium dioxide, and are mineral-based; the particles of these ingredients sit on top of the skin and block harmful UV rays. These ingredients are less harmful to corals and are not linked to coral bleaching.

Rigging: A general term for all the lines on a boat.

Rode: A rope, especially one securing an anchor or trawl.

Round bottom hull: A hull designed to be easily maneuverable but may tip easily.

Rod holder: Device designed to safely and securely hold fishing rods either vertically or horizontally.

Rudder: Located beneath the boat, the rudder is a flat piece of wood, fiberglass, or metal that is used to steer the ship. Larger sailboats control the rudder via a wheel, while smaller sailboats will have a steering mechanism directly aft, i.e., tiller.

Runabout: A small sporty craft intender for day cruising, water skiing, fishing.

Sabiki rig: A multi-lure rig (sizes 2 - 4) intended to catch multiple baitfish at one time. Sabikis consist of 6 to 10 small hooks.

Sailboat: A vessel that is operated by sail only. Since many sailboats are equipped with engines, they are considered powerboats when they are in use, even if their sails are up.

Scope: Length the anchor line or chain. The ratio to the length of anchor line to the depth of the water.

Seacock: Valve in the ship's hull through which seawater may pass.

Search and rescue (SAR:) The search for by the use of aircraft, surface craft, submarines, specialized rescue teams and equipment and provision of aid to people who are in distress or imminent danger on land or at sea.

Sécurité: The radio safety signal given on Channel 16. The signal announces a message about safety of navigation, or important weather warning.

Seelonce: Distress silence signal. A vessel in distress or station control of distress may impose silence on any station that interfere by sending *"Seelonce Mayday."*

Sheet: Line used to trim a sail.

Shipshape: In good order; trim and neat.

Shoal: A natural submerged ridge, bank, or bar that consists of, or is covered by, sand or other unconsolidated material, and rises from the bed of a body of water to near the surface.

Shroud: Mast support rigging, usually a wire, that runs from the mast to the side of the boat.

Skinny water: A thin amount of shallow water, up to five feet. This term is most often used with saltwater fishermen; refers to the very shallow flats of water in the Florida Keys.

Sonar: A method to locate objects and determine distance by transmitting sound waves through water and measuring the time it takes the echo to bounce back. Used in depth finders and fishfinders.

SPA Zone: A Sanctuary Protected Area – yellow mooring balls define the area. No: anchoring, fishing, standing, or touching is permissible in these areas

Spar: A general term for masts, yards and booms.

Spider hitch: Forms a double line or a loop in the line for light tackle fishing. It is easier and faster to tie than the Bimini twist but lacks the shock absorption capacity.

SPOT: A Satellite GPS Messenger provides a vital line of communication with friends and family when you want it, and emergency assistance when you need it.

Stand-on vessel: The boat the must continue on the same course and speed when following the Rules of the Road *(see give-way vessel).*

Starboard: The right side of a boat as you face forward.

Steerage: the act or practice of steering. A ship's steering mechanism.

Stern: The rear or back of a boat.

Strakes: Molded strips that run lengthwise along the hull bottom on modern planing boats.

Sustainable fishing: Leaving enough fish in the ocean, respecting habitats and ensuring people who depend on fishing can maintain their livelihoods.

Swivel: is a small device for fishing consisting of two rings connected to a pivoting joint. Usually made of metal, and the pivoting joint is usually ball, or barrel-shaped. Commonly used to tie a leader to fishing line.

Tack: *(Sailing)* To come about. The lower forward corner of the sail. Sailing with the wind on a given side, as in a starboard or port tack.

Tacking: *(Sailing)* The opposite of jibing, this basic sailing maneuver refers to turning the bow of the boat through the wind so that the wind changes from one side of the boat to the other side. The boom of a boat will always shift from one side to the other when performing a tack or a jibe.

Throat halyard (Throat): *(Sailing)* A line that raises the end of a gaff nearer to the mast, as opposed to the peak halyard which raises the end further from the mast.

Throttle: A mechanical part of the boat that regulates the speed of the engine.

Tide: The rise and fall of waters controlled by the gravitational pull of the moon and sun.

Tidal coefficient: The size of the tide in relation to its mean. The higher the tidal coefficient, the larger the tidal range – i.e. the difference in water height between high and low tide.

Top Spot: A fishing chart, similar to a navigation chart but not as specific, and showing fishing an dive spots.

Tracer: A port on an outboard engine where water is pumped through.

Transom: The outside of the boat's stern.

Trawl: an act of fishing with a trawl net (a large wide-mouthed fishing net dragged by a vessel along the bottom or in the midwater of the sea or a lake.)

Trim: The way a boat floats in relation to the horizon, bow up, bow down or even. To adjust a boat's horizontal running angle by directing the outboard or stern drive's thrust up or down. Also, to set a sail in correct relation to the wind.

Trim tabs: Hydraulically adjusted horizontal plates located on the bottom of the transom that control the trim angle of a boat at speed.

Trolling: To fish by towing an array of baited lines or lures behind the boat.

True wind: Direction and velocity of wind as measured on land, distinct from apparent wind.

Trucker's hitch: Used to cinch down a load. It allows a line to be pulled very tight. It is used by truckers to secure heavy loads in place and works equally well tying kayaks to the tops of cars.

Tuna tower: A tall tower used for spotting fish in the distance; often with a second set of helm controls.

T-top: A fixed shade above the center console of a boat; can be hard or canvas.

Twin propellers (Screws): A boat equipped with two engines and two propellers.

Twin outboard steering: Twin outboard motors have several advantages; power, back-up motor, and steering. Two motors enable the operator to effectively steer without using the steering wheel. If the port side control shifter is in forward and the starboard side shifter is in reverse, the boat will spin in a circle / on a dime to starboard. In the opposite scenario, the boat will spin in a circle to port. When perfected, one can land, dock, and steer more effectively.

Underway: When the boat is in motion. A vessel not at anchor, made fast to a pier, or aground.

Uni knot: A multi purpose fishing knot that can be used for attaching the fishing line to the arbor of a reel, for joining lines, and for attaching lures, snaps, and swivels.

VHF radio: The primary way for you to communicate while on the water; very high frequency; a bandwidth designation commonly used by marine radios.

Wake: The path left by a moving boat in the water; wave.

Waterline: Where the water meets the sides (and bow/stern) of the boat.

Waypoint: The coordinates of a specific location.

Winch: A hauling or lifting device consisting of a rope, cable, or chain winding around a horizontal rotating drum, turned by a crank or by motor or other power source; a windlass.

Windward: Toward the direction from which the wind is coming.

Working end: The end of the top opposite the bitter end that can be attached to and anchor or cleat.

Zinc anodes: Small pieces of zinc that attach to metal boat and engine components to help protect them from corrosion due to electrolysis.

www.ingramcontent.com/pod-product-compliance
Lightning Source LLC
Chambersburg PA
CBHW042135160426
43200CB00019B/2944